Intellectual
Property Rights

Other Books in the Issues on Trial Series:

Domestic Violence

Hate Crimes

Juvenile Justice

Medical Rights

Political Corruption

Pollution

The War on Drugs

White-Collar Crime

Intellectual Property Rights

Sylvia Engdahl, Book Editor

GREENHAVEN PRESS
A part of Gale, Cengage Learning

GALE
CENGAGE Learning™

Detroit • New York • San Francisco • New Haven, Conn • Waterville, Maine • London

GALE
CENGAGE Learning™

Christine Nasso, *Publisher*
Elizabeth Des Chenes, *Managing Editor*

© 2010 Greenhaven Press, a part of Gale, Cengage Learning

For more information, contact:
Greenhaven Press
27500 Drake Rd.
Farmington Hills, MI 48331-3535
Or you can visit our Internet site at gale.cengage.com.

For product information and technology assistance, contact us at

Gale Customer Support, 1-800-877-4253
For permission to use material from this text or product, submit all requests online at www.cengage.com/permissions

Further permissions questions can be emailed to permissionrequest@cengage.com

Articles in Greenhaven Press anthologies are often edited for length to meet page requirements. In addition, original titles of these works are changed to clearly present the main thesis and to explicitly indicate the author's opinion. Every effort is made to ensure that Greenhaven Press accurately reflects the original intent of the authors. Every effort has been made to trace the owners of copyrighted material.

Cover photograph reproduced by permission of Nicholas Kamm/AFP/Getty Images.

LIBRARY OF CONGRESS CATALOGING-IN-PUBLICATION DATA

Intellectual property rights / Sylvia Engdahl, book editor.
    p. cm. -- (Issues on trial)
  Includes bibliographical references and index.
  ISBN-13: 978-0-7377-4489-7 (hardcover)
  1. Copyright--United States. 2. Intellectual property--United States. I. Engdahl, Sylvia.
  KF2995.I55 2009
  346.7304'8--dc22

2009018273

Printed in the United States of America
1 2 3 4 5 6 7 13 12 11 10 09

Contents

Foreword   11

Introduction   14

Chapter 1: Home Videotaping of Television Shows Docs Not Violate Copyright Law

Case Overview: *Sony Corporation of America*   19
v. Universal City Studios (1984)

1. Majority Opinion: Home Taping of Television   22
   Shows Is Not an Infringement of Copyright
   John Paul Stevens

   By a single vote, the Supreme Court ruled that it is not
   an infringement of copyright for consumers to record
   television shows on VCRs and that VCRs can therefore
   be sold to the public, a decision that had tremendous
   significance in the development of media technology.

2. Dissenting Opinion: Home Taping of Television   33
   Shows Is a Violation of Copyright Law
   Harry Blackmun

   Justice Blackmun argues that making copies of television
   shows does violate the copyright law and that the only
   way to balance the interests of movie studios, VCR manufacturers, and the public would be for Congress to address the issue.

3. Home Taping of Television Shows   45
   Is Not Fair Use
   Irwin Karp

   An attorney argues that recording television shows on
   VCRs does not come under the Fair Use exception to
   copyright laws because it puts copyrighted works into
   the hands of the public without either the permission of
   authors and dramatists or any compensation to them.

4. The Supreme Court Debated Home Taping
   of Television Shows at Length   52
   Jonathan Band and Andrew J. McLaughlin

   Lawyers describe the compromises reached by the justices
   of the Supreme Court during a full year of debate about
   Sony v. Universal, as revealed by papers of Justice Thurgood Marshall that were made public after his death.

5. The Precedent Set by *Sony v. Universal*   64
   Has Resulted in Illegal Downloading
   Marci Hamilton

   A law professor argues that the precedent set by *Sony v.
   Universal* has led to the Internet posting of illegal video
   copies of television shows and movies that viewers would
   otherwise pay to see, and that the decision should be reversed.

Chapter 2: News Media May Not Use Unpublished Material Without Permission

Case Overview: *Harper & Row,*   70
Publishers, Inc. v. Nation Enterprises (1985)

1. Majority Opinion: Newsworthiness Does   72
   Not Justify Copyright Violation
   Sandra Day O'Connor

   The Supreme Court ruled that it was a violation of copyright for *The Nation* magazine to print an unpublished
   excerpt from President Gerald Ford's memoirs—which
   he had sold to another publisher—even though it was
   newsworthy.

2. Dissenting Opinion: Publication of the Disputed   82
   Material Was Fair Use
   William J. Brennan

   Justice Brennan argues that the Court's definition of fair
   use is too narrow and that it will stifle the broad dissemination of ideas and information copyright is intended to nurture.

3. The Court Protected Commercial Interests   **94**
at the Expense of Free Dissemination of Facts
Slade Metcalf

An attorney explains how the Supreme Court evaluates
fair use and what impact can be expected from its ruling,
which he feels protected commercial interests at the expense of the free and open dissemination of facts.

4. The Right to Free Speech Includes a Right   **101**
to Choose Where to Speak
George F. Will

A well-known columnist argues that the editor who
printed material without permission was hypocritical in
claiming that the First Amendment overrides commercial
interests because in order to sell magazines, he denied
the author the freedom to choose when and where to
publish.

5. The Fair Use Exemption to Copyright Depends   **105**
on Factors Specific to Each Case
Jack Shafer

A journalist argues that Hillary Clinton and J.K. Rowling,
both of whom considered suing the press for publishing
quotations from their books prior to publication, did not
have a good case because *Harper & Row v. Nation* is not
as firm a precedent as it is commonly said to be.

Chapter 3: The Copyright Term Extension Act of 1998 Is Not Unconstitutional

Case Overview: *Eldred v. Ashcroft* (2003)   **113**

1. Majority Opinion: Congress Has the Authority   **115**
to Set the Copyright Term
Ruth Bader Ginsburg

The Supreme Court ruled that Congress had the power
to pass the Sonny Bono Copyright Term Extension Act,
extending the term of copyright for existing works, and
that this did not interfere with the principle of free
speech.

2. Dissenting Opinion: The Copyright Term   **124**
Extension Act Is Unconstitutional
Stephen Breyer

Justice Breyer argues that under the Constitution the
purpose of copyright is to promote the progress of
knowledge and learning not only by creating incentives
for authors to produce, but by removing restrictions on
dissemination of their work after its copyright expires,
and also increasing the length of the copyright term will
result in serious harm to the public.

3. The Copyright Term Extension Act Was   **134**
Opposed by Scholars and Libraries
Andrea L. Foster

Eric Eldred, a retired computer expert who ran an award-
winning Web site on which he made classic literature
freely available to the public, was the plaintiff in *Eldred v.
Ashcroft*. Many scholarly and library groups supported
his suit, which was opposed by large media companies.

4. The Copyright Term Extension Act Does   **144**
Not Serve the Purpose of Copyright
David Bollier

A public policy analyst argues that copyright laws exist to
encourage creative work and that the Copyright Extension Act, which was passed because the Walt Disney
Company lobbied Congress in order to keep the copyright on Mickey Mouse from expiring, benefits only large
media corporations and the heirs of dead authors.

Chapter 4: Distributing Software Intended for Illegal File-Sharing Violates Copyright Law

Case Overview: *Metro-Goldwyn-Mayer*   **152**
Studios, Inc. v. Grokster, Ltd. (2005)

1. Unanimous Opinion: Companies That   **154**
Encourage Illegal File-Sharing Are Liable
for Copyright Infringement
David Souter

The Supreme Court ruled that a company that distributes file-sharing software with the object of promoting its use to infringe copyright is liable for the resulting acts of infringement by people who use that software, even if it also has lawful uses.

2. File-Sharing Networks Hurt Artists and   165
   Discourage the Creation of New Works
   Richard K. Armey

   A former U.S. House majority leader argues that downloading music without paying for it is stealing, that it victimizes artists and recording technicians, and that if peer-to-peer networks are allowed to continue they will sacrifice the incentive for creative individuals to invest in their art.

3. Some Artists Believe File-Sharing Networks   169
   Help Them
   Jonathan Krim

   Some musicians and artists oppose the recording studios' desire to shut down peer-to-peer file-sharing networks because they believe such services give their work exposure and provide an alternate way for them to distribute it.

4. Holding Companies Liable for Users' Copyright   173
   Violations Discourages Internet Technology
   Heather S. Hall

   A law student argues that the Supreme Court ruling that finds file-sharing software providers liable for their users' copyright infringement will stifle future Internet innovations and that the Supreme Court should not have reversed the lower court's decision about the Grokster network.

5. The *Grokster* Decision Will Not Prevent   180
   the Development of File-Sharing Technology
   Pamela Samuelson

   A law professor explains that although MGM won the *Grokster* case, it did not get what the entertainment industry had hoped for because the Court did not overturn the *Sony* decision, which protects developers of technology capable of some noninfringing uses.

Organizations to Contact   **190**

For Further Research   **196**

Index   **201**

Foreword

The U.S. courts have long served as a battleground for the most highly charged and contentious issues of the time. Divisive matters are often brought into the legal system by activists who feel strongly for their cause and demand an official resolution. Indeed, subjects that give rise to intense emotions or involve closely held religious or moral beliefs lay at the heart of the most polemical court rulings in history. One such case was *Brown v. Board of Education* (1954), which ended racial segregation in schools. Prior to *Brown*, the courts had held that blacks could be forced to use separate facilities as long as these facilities were equal to that of whites.

For years many groups had opposed segregation based on religious, moral, and legal grounds. Educators produced heartfelt testimony that segregated schooling greatly disadvantaged black children. They noted that in comparison to whites, blacks received a substandard education in deplorable conditions. Religious leaders such as Martin Luther King Jr. preached that the harsh treatment of blacks was immoral and unjust. Many involved in civil rights law, such as Thurgood Marshall, called for equal protection of all people under the law, as their study of the Constitution had indicated that segregation was illegal and un-American. Whatever their motivation for ending the practice, and despite the threats they received from segregationists, these ardent activists remained unwavering in their cause.

Those fighting against the integration of schools were mainly white southerners who did not believe that whites and blacks should intermingle. Blacks were subordinate to whites, they maintained, and society had to resist any attempt to break down strict color lines. Some white southerners charged that segregated schooling was *not* hindering blacks' education. For example, Virginia attorney general J. Lindsay Almond asserted, "With the help and the sympathy and the love and re-spect of the white people of the South, the colored man has risen under that educational process to a place of eminence and respect throughout the nation. It has served him well." So when the Supreme Court ruled against the segregationists in *Brown*, the South responded with vociferous cries of protest. Even government leaders criticized the decision. The governor of Arkansas, Orval Faubus, stated that he would not "be a party to any attempt to force acceptance of change to which the people are so overwhelmingly opposed." Indeed, resistance to integration was so great that when black students arrived at the formerly all-white Central High School in Arkansas, fed-eral troops had to be dispatched to quell a threatening mob of protesters.

Nevertheless, the *Brown* decision was enforced and the South integrated its schools. In this instance, the Court, while not settling the issue to everyone's satisfaction, functioned as an instrument of progress by forcing a major social change. Historian David Halberstam observes that the *Brown* ruling "deprived segregationist practices of their moral legitimacy. . . . It was therefore perhaps the single most important moment of the decade, the moment that separated the old order from the new and helped create the tumultuous era just arriving." Considered one of the most important victories for civil rights, *Brown* paved the way for challenges to racial segregation in many areas, including on public buses and in restaurants.

In examining *Brown*, it becomes apparent that the courts play an influential role—and face an arduous challenge—in shaping the debate over emotionally charged social issues. Judges must balance competing interests, keeping in mind the high stakes and intense emotions on both sides. As exempli-fied by *Brown*, judicial decisions often upset the status quo and initiate significant changes in society. Greenhaven Press's Issues on Trial series captures the controversy surrounding in-fluential court rulings and explores the social ramifications of such decisions from varying perspectives. Each anthology highlights one social issue—such as the death penalty, students' rights, or wartime civil liberties. Each volume then focuses on key historical and contemporary court cases that helped mold the issue as we know it today. The books include a compendium of primary sources—court rulings, dissents, and immediate reactions to the rulings—as well as secondary sources from experts in the field, people involved in the cases, legal analysts, and other commentators opining on the implications and legacy of the chosen cases. An annotated table of contents, an in-depth introduction, and prefaces that overview each case all provide context as readers delve into the topic at hand. To help students fully probe the subject, each volume contains book and periodical bibliographies, a comprehensive index, and a list of organizations to contact. With these features, the Issues on Trial series offers a well-rounded perspective on the courts' role in framing society's thorniest, most impassioned debates.

Introduction

Intellectual property (IP) is a legal term referring to rights over creations of the mind, including both literary or artistic creations—such as books, music, and paintings—and commercial creations. The major types of intellectual property are copyrights, patents, and trademarks. Laws relating to IP give the creator of a work the exclusive right to authorize its reproduction for a set period of time. The purpose of such laws is to encourage creation of new literary, artistic, and informational works for the ultimate benefit of society. The copyright clause of the U.S. Constitution empowers Congress "to promote the Progress of Science [knowledge] and useful Arts, by securing for limited Times to Authors and Inventors the exclusive Right to their respective Writings and Discoveries." If creators were not given this right, they could not earn money from their work, and some would be unable or unwilling to devote time to it.

Writers, artists, or inventors can sell some or all of their rights to a company that is equipped to market their works in exchange for a fee or a percentage of the profits. Or, they may be hired by a company to produce a certain work, known as a work for hire, in which case the rights belong to that company. For example, writers commonly sell rights to publishers, and musicians sell them to record labels, while patents often belong to the inventor's employer. (With some forms of IP, such as movies or television broadcasts, the rights belong to a company in the first place; this is also the case with trademarks.) When exclusive rights are owned by a company, the creator has no control over the work's reproduction, although he or she receives the money (royalty) that has been agreed upon. An author, for instance, cannot personally grant permission for someone to make copies of work to which all rights have been sold to a publisher.

Why would an author or artist give up control over his or her own work? In the case of someone who is famous, a lot of money may be paid for the rights, but most writers and musicians are not famous and receive very little money. They transfer their rights to publishers and record labels because they want their work to reach an audience, whether or not they hope that this will result in their becoming rich and famous later on. Traditionally, only companies have been in a position to get literary or artistic work into the hands of large audiences. Today, new technologies are enabling authors to self-publish and independent musicians to produce recordings on their own, but works made available in that way may reach very few people compared with the number who buy copies from a publisher or record label.

Companies cannot invest in new creative works that they do not have an exclusive right to market, since that would mean others could reap the profits from the investment. Production and distribution of books and music is very costly. For example, 40 to 55 percent of the retail price of a book goes neither to the author nor to the publisher but to the distributor and/or retail seller. Since besides paying the author the publisher must spend large sums on editing, cover art, printing, and advertising, this leaves little profit on each book, and publishers would not stay in business if they made no profit at all. Yet if there were no publishing companies, authors would have no way to make their work known to the general public. Even if they went on creating it privately—which some would not do—it could not be widely distributed.

Recently, there has been controversy over whether copyright is a good idea. Some people believe that all creative works should be in the public domain—that is, legal to copy without permission—either from the time of their creation or after a very short period. Others point out that if this were true, publishers, record labels, and movie studios would go out of business and no more creative works would be issued. Even if writers, artists, and filmmakers posted their own works on the Internet, in most cases not enough people would become aware of them for the authors to receive much recognition. Quite a lot of good fiction and music has been independently posted by its creators, and yet rarely do people become aware of any single work—the popular works are usually those that have been financially backed and publicized by companies.

This is why the majority of Americans believe that copyright is an important stimulus for creativity, and it also explains why piracy is harmful. It is sometimes said that popular recording stars are rich and that very little of the price of a CD goes to the artist in any case, so it does not really hurt musicians when people download illegal copies of copyrighted music. But the harm is not just in loss of profits from particular copies. The danger is that so many illegal copies are being made that if the trend continues, the recording labels may not make enough profit to go on producing new works. Established artists will then be unable to issue new releases, new artists will not have an opportunity to reach large audiences, and the general public will be deprived of the benefit of those artists' talents.

On the other hand, some people believe that there are problems with the present system that need to be solved. Many of them download music not to avoid paying for what they like, but for convenience and because they prefer newer technologies, such as MP3 players, to CDs or want to choose individual songs rather than whole albums. More and more copyrighted recordings are being made legally available for a fee, but not all that the public wants to obtain. It has been suggested that the recording industry has not kept pace with technology—that it is fighting a losing battle in assuming that the sale of physical media will always be the primary method of music distribution, and that it should find a way of paying artists that does not depend on such media.

Problems also exist in connection with literary copyrights. Some people question whether copyrights should extend to the heirs of dead authors, as Congress originally intended and reaffirmed in 1998 through the passage of the Copyright Term Extension Act. Now that it is possible to make archived texts available electronically, many feel that the public should not have to pay for works that need no expensive distribution to become recognized. Furthermore, libraries and other producers of text databases are having difficulty obtaining permission to use old texts because authors of out-of-print works (or their heirs), whose publishers no longer hold the rights, often cannot be located. In addition, as traditional publishers focus more and more on best-selling authors and other writers turn to e-book publishing, the problem of how to protect the rights of e-book authors is growing.

All in all, the issues surrounding copyright today are very different from any imagined at the time copyright laws were originally written. Two of the Supreme Court cases discussed in this book deal with direct conflicts between traditional views of copyright and new technologies. The other two involve situations that could not have arisen before the rapid dissemination and widespread availability of copyrighted works became common. Although patents and trademarks are also intellectual property and are also impacted by technological change, the book focuses on copyright law because copyright issues are the ones ordinary people most often encounter in their daily lives.

CHAPTER 1

Home Videotaping of Television Shows Does Not Violate Copyright Law

Case Overview

Sony Corporation of America v. Universal City Studios (1984)

The home recording of television programs—and even the viewing of prerecorded movies in homes—is a relatively recent development. Until the late 1970s, TV shows, including old movies, could only be seen at the time they were aired. Seeing two programs run in the same time slot was not possible, unless the unwatched program was later rerun. Movies not broadcast could be seen only in theaters. And if it had not been for a landmark case that was decided by only one vote in the Supreme Court, that might still be true today.

The first VCR (videocassette recorder)—then called a VTR (videotape recorder)—to be successfully marketed was the Betamax, manufactured by the Sony Corporation. The technology was unfamiliar to the public, and the first machines were expensive, so not many homes had them; but it was obvious that they were going to catch on. It was not long before the movie studios realized that people were making copies of material that was copyrighted, and that more and more would do so in the future. Reproducing copyrighted works is, of course, against the law, except when it can be considered "fair use." The studios did not think the copying of movies or TV series was fair use. They licensed them only for specific showings and believed people should not be allowed to see them repeatedly without paying. They feared it might decrease the size of the audiences that determined ratings and advertising rates or limit the market for reruns. As there was no way they could catch people making tapes in their own homes, they filed suit against Sony, hoping to stop the sale of the Betamax.

Sony itself had not broken the copyright law, so Universal sued on the grounds that because Sony knew its machines were used to tape copyrighted programs, it was "contributing" to copyright infringement. In 1979, after three years of litigation, the district court ruled in favor of Sony, stating that "noncommercial home-use recording of material broadcast over the public airwaves" qualified as fair use because there was no evidence that it would cause any loss to the studios. "The new technology of videotape recording does bring uncertainty and change which, quite naturally, induce fear," the court's opinion stated. "History, however, shows that this fear may be misplaced."

After another two years, however, the appeals court reversed the district court's decision. Sony then appealed to the Supreme Court. The justices of the Supreme Court found it an especially difficult case to decide, so they took the unusual step of hearing oral arguments from the lawyers for a second time. They debated for a whole year, not reaching a decision until 1984. By this time home taping was widespread; the Betamax had been on the market for eight years and had been joined by competing VCRs. It would have been difficult to stop their sale, but some justices felt the machines should be made incapable of recording broadcasts, that some sort of technological copy protection might be developed or that licensing of VCRs to enable the charging of royalties might be possible. If any of these things had happened, people's viewing options would have become very different from what they are now. There might not be so many channels if only live watching were possible. It is not even certain that the video rental business—which has greatly benefited the studios—would have developed, because people might not have bought VCRs that could not record as well as play back tapes.

In the end, the Supreme Court ruled five to four in Sony's favor—just one vote determined the course of entertainment technology's future. The principle on which the ruling was based established a precedent that not only permitted the videotaping of broadcasts, but also influenced the downloading of copyrighted material from the Internet (see Chapter 4 of this book). The majority of the Court held that if a device was capable of significant uses that did not infringe copyright, the manufacturer was not liable for its users' infringement, and it considered the time-shifting of television programs a noninfringing use.

> "One may search the Copyright Act in vain for any sign that the elected representatives of the millions of people who watch television every day have made it unlawful to copy a program for later viewing at home."

Majority Opinion: Home Taping of Television Shows Is Not an Infringement of Copyright

John Paul Stevens

John Paul Stevens is, as of 2009, the oldest and longest-serving member of the U.S. Supreme Court, and he is generally considered to be the leader of its liberal faction. The following opinion that he wrote in Sony v. Universal Studios *presents the Court's reasons for deciding that Sony, the manufacturer of the Betamax VCR (then called a VTR), was not responsible for users' copyright infringement, even though the company was aware that people were taping copyrighted TV programs. VCRs can also be used to tape programs that are not copyrighted, he points out, and to prohibit their sale would prevent this. Moreover, even the taping of copyrighted programs may be "fair use" under the copyright law. There is no evidence that home taping affects the market for those programs—it is done mainly for time-shifting (to watch at one's leisure), which the Court considers fair use because it is not detrimental to copyright holders. If a technology is capable of substantial noninfringing uses, then a company that*

John Paul Stevens, majority opinion, *Sony Corporation of America v. Universal City Studios*, U.S. Supreme Court, January 17, 1984.

sells it is not liable for contributing to copyright infringement, Justice Stevens says, and he finds nothing in the copyright law that makes time-shifting illegal.

The District Court concluded that noncommercial home use recording of material broadcast over the public airwaves was a fair use of copyrighted works, and did not constitute copyright infringement. It emphasized the fact that the material was broadcast free to the public at large, the noncommercial character of the use, and the private character of the activity conducted entirely within the home. Moreover, the court found that the purpose of this use served the public interest in increasing access to television programming, an interest that "is consistent with the First Amendment policy of providing the fullest possible access to information through the public airwaves." Even when an entire copyrighted work was recorded, the District Court regarded the copying as fair use "because there is no accompanying reduction in the market for 'plaintiff's original work.'"

As an independent ground of decision, the District Court also concluded that Sony could not be held liable as a contributory infringer even if the home use of a VTR [videotape recorder] was considered an infringing use. The District Court noted that Sony had no direct involvement with any Betamax purchasers who recorded copyrighted works off the air. Sony's advertising was silent on the subject of possible copyright infringement, but its instruction booklet contained the following statement: "Television programs, films, videotapes and other materials may be copyrighted. Unauthorized recording of such material may be contrary to the provisions of the United States copyright laws."

The District Court assumed that Sony had constructive knowledge of the probability that the Betamax machine would be used to record copyrighted programs, but found that Sony merely sold a "product capable of a variety of uses, some of them allegedly infringing." It reasoned:

Selling a staple article of commerce—*e.g.*, a typewriter, a recorder, a camera, a photocopying machine—technically contributes to any infringing use subsequently made thereof, but this kind of "contribution," if deemed sufficient as a basis for liability, would expand the theory beyond precedent, and arguably beyond judicial management.

... Commerce would indeed be hampered if manufacturers of staple items were held liable as contributory infringers whenever they "constructively" knew that some purchasers on some occasions would use their product for a purpose which a court later deemed, as a matter of first impression, to be an infringement.

Finally, the District Court discussed the respondents' prayer for injunctive relief, noting that they had asked for an injunction either preventing the future sale of Betamax machines or requiring that the machines be rendered incapable of recording copyrighted works off the air. The court stated that it had "found no case in which the manufacturers, distributors, retailers and advertisers of the instrument enabling the infringement were sued by the copyright holders," and that the request for relief in this case "is unique."

It concluded that an injunction was wholly inappropriate because any possible harm to respondents was outweighed by the fact that "the Betamax could still legally be used to record noncopyrighted material or material whose owners consented to the copying. An injunction would deprive the public of the ability to use the Betamax for this noninfringing off-the-air recording."

The Court of Appeals' Decision

The Court of Appeals reversed the District Court's judgment on respondents' copyright claim. It did not set aside any of the District Court's findings of fact. Rather, it concluded as a matter of law that the home use of a VTR was not a fair use, because it was not a "productive use." It therefore held that it was unnecessary for plaintiffs to prove any harm to the potential market for the copyrighted works, but then observed that it seemed clear that the cumulative effect of mass reproduction made possible by VTR's would tend to diminish the potential market for respondents' works.

On the issue of contributory infringement, the Court of Appeals first rejected the analogy to staple articles of commerce such as tape recorders or photocopying machines. It noted that such machines "may have substantial benefit for some purposes" and do not "even remotely raise copyright problems." VTR's, however, are sold "for the primary purpose of reproducing television programming," and "[v]irtually all" such programming is copyrighted material. The Court of Appeals concluded, therefore, that VTR's were not suitable for any substantial noninfringing use even if some copyright owners elect not to enforce their rights.

The Court of Appeals also rejected the District Court's reliance on Sony's lack of knowledge that home use constituted infringement. Assuming that the statutory provisions defining the remedies for infringement applied also to the nonstatutory tort [act for which one can be sued] of contributory infringement, the court stated that a defendant's good faith would merely reduce his damages liability, but would not excuse the infringing conduct. It held that Sony was chargeable with knowledge of the homeowner's infringing activity because the reproduction of copyrighted materials was either "the most conspicuous use" or "the major use" of the Betamax product.

On the matter of relief, the Court of Appeals concluded that "statutory damages may be appropriate" and that the District Court should reconsider its determination that an injunction would not be an appropriate remedy; and, referring to "the analogous photocopying area," suggested that a continuing royalty pursuant to a judicially created compulsory license may very well be an acceptable resolution of the relief issue. . . .

Legislative Response to New Technologies

As the text of the Constitution makes plain, it is Congress that has been assigned the task of defining the scope of the limited monopoly that should be granted to authors or to inventors in order to give the public appropriate access to their work product. Because this task involves a difficult balance between the interests of authors and inventors in the control and exploitation of their writings and discoveries on the one hand, and society's competing interest in the free flow of ideas, information, and commerce on the other hand, our patent and copyright statutes have been amended repeatedly.

From its beginning, the law of copyright has developed in response to significant changes in technology. Indeed, it was the invention of a new form of copying equipment—the printing press—that gave rise to the original need for copyright protection. Repeatedly, as new developments have occurred in this country, it has been the Congress that has fashioned the new rules that new technology made necessary. . . .

Sound policy, as well as history, supports our consistent deference to Congress when major technological innovations alter the market for copyrighted materials. Congress has the constitutional authority and the institutional ability to accommodate fully the varied permutations of competing interests that are inevitably implicated by such new technology.

In a case like this, in which Congress has not plainly marked our course, we must be circumspect in construing the scope of rights created by a legislative enactment which never contemplated such a calculus of interests. . . .

The two respondents in this case do not seek relief against the Betamax users who have allegedly infringed their copyrights. Moreover, this is not a class action on behalf of all copyright owners who license their works for television broadcast, and respondents have no right to invoke whatever rights other copyright holders may have to bring infringement actions based on Betamax copying of their works. As was made clear by their own evidence, the copying of the respondents' programs represents a small portion of the total use of VTR's. It is, however, the taping of respondents' own copyrighted programs that provides them with standing to charge Sony with contributory infringement. To prevail, they have the burden of proving that users of the Betamax have infringed their copyrights, and that Sony should be held responsible for that infringement. . . .

Sony in the instant [present] case does not supply Betamax consumers with respondents' works; respondents do. Sony supplies a piece of equipment that is generally capable of copying the entire range of programs that may be televised: those that are uncopyrighted, those that are copyrighted but may be copied without objection from the copyright holder, and those that the copyright holder would prefer not to have copied. . . .

If vicarious liability is to be imposed on Sony in this case, it must rest on the fact that it has sold equipment with constructive knowledge of the fact that its customers may use that equipment to make unauthorized copies of copyrighted material. There is no precedent in the law of copyright for the imposition of vicarious liability on such a theory. . . .

The question is thus whether the Betamax is capable of commercially significant noninfringing uses. In order to resolve that question, we need not explore *all* the different potential uses of the machine and determine whether or not they would constitute infringement. Rather, we need only consider whether, on the basis of the facts as found by the District Court, a significant number of them would be noninfringing. Moreover, in order to resolve this case, we need not give precise content to the question of how much use is commercially significant. For one potential use of the Betamax plainly satisfies this standard, however it is understood: private, noncommercial time-shifting in the home. It does so both (A) because respondents have no right to prevent other

copyright holders from authorizing it for their programs, and
(B) because the District Court's factual findings reveal that
even the unauthorized home time-shifting of respondents'
programs is legitimate fair use.

Authorized Time-Shifting

Each of the respondents owns a large inventory of valuable
copyrights, but, in the total spectrum of television programming, their combined market share is small. The exact percentage is not specified, but it is well below 10%. If they were
to prevail, the outcome of this litigation would have a significant impact on both the producers and the viewers of the remaining 90% of the programming in the Nation. No doubt,
many other producers share respondents' concern about the
possible consequences of unrestricted copying. Nevertheless
the findings of the District Court make it clear that time-
shifting may enlarge the total viewing audience, and that many
producers are willing to allow private time-shifting to continue, at least for an experimental time period.

The District Court found:

> Even if it were deemed that home-use recording of copy-
> righted material constituted infringement, the Betamax
> could still legally be used to record noncopyrighted material
> or material whose owners consented to the copying. An in-
> junction would deprive the public of the ability to use the
> Betamax for this noninfringing off-the-air recording. . . .

If there are millions of owners of VTR's who make copies
of televised sports events, religious broadcasts, and educational programs such as *Mister Rogers' Neighborhood*, and if
the proprietors of those programs welcome the practice, the
business of supplying the equipment that makes such copying
feasible should not be stifled simply because the equipment is
used by some individuals to make unauthorized reproductions
of respondents' works. The respondents do not represent a

class composed of all copyright holders. Yet a finding of contributory infringement would inevitably frustrate the interests of broadcasters in reaching the portion of their audience that is available only through time-shifting.

Of course, the fact that other copyright holders may welcome the practice of time-shifting does not mean that respondents should be deemed to have granted a license to copy their programs. Third-party conduct would be wholly irrelevant in an action for direct infringement of respondents' copyrights. But in an action for *contributory* infringement against the seller of copying equipment, the copyright holder may not prevail unless the relief that he seeks affects only his programs, or unless he speaks for virtually all copyright holders with an interest in the outcome. In this case, the record makes it perfectly clear that there are many important producers of national and local television programs who find nothing objectionable about the enlargement in the size of the television audience that results from the practice of time-shifting for private home use. The seller of the equipment that expands those producers' audiences cannot be a contributory infringer if, as is true in this case, it has had no direct involvement with any infringing activity.

Unauthorized Time-Shifting

Even unauthorized uses of a copyrighted work are not necessarily infringing. An unlicensed use of the copyright is not an infringement unless it conflicts with one of the specific exclusive rights conferred by the copyright statute. . . .

If the Betamax were used to make copies for a commercial or profitmaking purpose, such use would presumptively be unfair. The contrary presumption is appropriate here, however, because the District Court's findings plainly establish that time-shifting for private home use must be characterized as a noncommercial, nonprofit activity. Moreover, when one considers the nature of a televised copyrighted audiovisual work and that time-shifting merely enables a viewer to see such a work which he had been invited to witness in its entirety free of charge, the fact that the entire work is reproduced does not have its ordinary effect of militating against a finding of fair use.

This is not, however, the end of the inquiry, because Congress has also directed us to consider "the effect of the use upon the potential market for or value of the copyrighted work." The purpose of copyright is to create incentives for creative effort. Even copying for noncommercial purposes may impair the copyright holder's ability to obtain the rewards that Congress intended him to have. But a use that has no demonstrable effect upon the potential market for, or the value of, the copyrighted work need not be prohibited in order to protect the author's incentive to create. The prohibition of such noncommercial uses would merely inhibit access to ideas without any countervailing benefit.

Thus, although every commercial use of copyrighted material is presumptively an unfair exploitation of the monopoly privilege that belongs to the owner of the copyright, noncommercial uses are a different matter. A challenge to a noncommercial use of a copyrighted work requires proof either that the particular use is harmful or that, if it should become widespread, it would adversely affect the potential market for the copyrighted work. Actual present harm need not be shown; such a requirement would leave the copyright holder with no defense against predictable damage. Nor is it necessary to show with certainty that future harm will result. What is necessary is a showing by a preponderance of the evidence that some meaningful likelihood of future harm exists. If the intended use is for commercial gain, that likelihood may be presumed. But if it is for a noncommercial purpose, the likelihood must be demonstrated.

In this case, respondents failed to carry their burden with regard to home time-shifting. . . .

On the question of potential future harm from time-shifting, the District Court offered a more detailed analysis of the evidence. It rejected respondents' "fear that persons 'watching' the original telecast of a program will not be measured in the live audience, and the ratings and revenues will decrease" by observing that current measurement technology allows the Betamax audience to be reflected. It rejected respondents' prediction "that live television or movie audiences will decrease as more people watch Betamax tapes as an alternative," with the observation that "[t]here is no factual basis for [the underlying] assumption." It rejected respondents' "fear that time-shifting will reduce audiences for telecast re-runs," and concluded instead that "given current market practices, this should aid plaintiffs, rather than harm them." And it declared that respondents' suggestion that "theater or film rental exhibition of a program will suffer because of time-shifting recording of that program" "lacks merit." . . .

Time-Shifting Is Fair Use

The District Court's conclusions are buttressed by the fact that to the extent time-shifting expands public access to freely broadcast television programs, it yields societal benefits. In *Community Television of Southern California v. Gottfried*, we acknowledged the public interest in making television broadcasting more available [especially to hard-of-hearing viewers]. Concededly, that interest is not unlimited. But it supports an interpretation of the concept of "fair use" that requires the copyright holder to demonstrate some likelihood of harm before he may condemn a private act of time-shifting as a violation of federal law.

When these factors are all weighed in the "equitable rule of reason" balance, we must conclude that this record amply supports the District Court's conclusion that home time-shifting is fair use. In light of the findings of the District Court regarding the state of the empirical data, it is clear that the Court of Appeals erred in holding that the statute as presently written bars such conduct. . . .

One may search the Copyright Act in vain for any sign that the elected representatives of the millions of people who watch television every day have made it unlawful to copy a program for later viewing at home, or have enacted a flat prohibition against the sale of machines that make such copying possible.

It may well be that Congress will take a fresh look at this new technology, just as it so often has examined other innovations in the past. But it is not our job to apply laws that have not yet been written. Applying the copyright statute, as it now reads, to the facts as they have been developed in this case, the judgment of the Court of Appeals must be reversed.

> "Time-shifting is noncommercial in the same sense that stealing jewelry and wearing it—instead of reselling it—is noncommercial. Purely consumptive uses are certainly not what the fair use doctrine was designed to protect."

Dissenting Opinion: Home Taping of Television Shows Is a Violation of Copyright Law

Harry Blackmun

Harry Blackmun was a justice of the Supreme Court from 1970 to 1994. He is best known as the author of the majority opinion in Roe v. Wade, *the decision that overturned laws prohibiting abortion. In the following dissenting opinion in* Sony v. Universal Studios, *he maintains that home taping of television shows is an infringement of copyright and that the Court should have found Sony, the manufacturer of the Betamax videorecorder, liable. In his opinion, even though the Betamax was capable of noninfringing uses, it was intended mainly for reproducing copyrighted works and Sony knew that was what it was used for, so selling it contributed to illegal activity. Blackmun disagrees with the Court's ruling that taping for time-shifting falls under the "fair use" exception to the copyright law and thus is not illegal. He argues that fair use means a productive use—one in which part of a work is used in some way during the production of a new creative work—and that it does not apply to purely consumptive uses such as watching television, especially not when a*

Harry Blackmun, dissenting opinion, *Sony Corporation of America v. Universal City Studios*, U.S. Supreme Court, January 17, 1984.

*whole work is copied. The demand for time-shifting capability
has created a new market for copyrighted works, he says, and the
profit should go to their creators rather than to Sony.*

The introduction of the home videotape recorder (VTR)
upon the market has enabled millions of Americans to
make recordings of television programs in their homes, for future and repeated viewing at their own convenience. While
this practice has proved highly popular with owners of television sets and VTR's, it understandably has been a matter of
concern for the holders of copyrights in the recorded programs. A result is the present litigation, raising the issues
whether the home recording of a copyrighted television program is an infringement of the copyright, and, if so, whether
the manufacturers and distributors of VTR's are liable as contributory infringers. I would hope that these questions ultimately will be considered seriously and in depth by the Congress and be resolved there, despite the fact that the Court's
decision today provides little incentive for congressional action. Our task in the meantime, however, is to resolve these issues as best we can in the light of ill-fitting existing copyright
law. . . .

Motion pictures and other audiovisual works have been
accorded full copyright protection since at least 1912, and
perhaps before. Congress continued this protection in the
1976 [Copyright] Act. Unlike the sound recording rights created by the 1971 Amendment, the reproduction rights associated with motion pictures under [Section] 106(1) are not
limited to reproduction for *public* distribution; the copyright
owner's right to reproduce the work exists independently,
and the "mere duplication of a copy may constitute an infringement even if it is never distributed." Moreover, the 1976
Act was intended as a comprehensive treatment of all aspects
of copyright law. The Reports accompanying the 1976 Act,
unlike the 1971 House Report, contain no suggestion that
home-use recording is somehow outside the scope of this all-

inclusive statute. It was clearly the intent of Congress that no additional exemptions were to be implied.

I therefore find in the 1976 Act no implied exemption to cover the home taping of television programs, whether it be for a single copy, for private use, or for home use. Taping a copyrighted television program is infringement unless it is permitted by the fair use exemption contained in [Section] 107 of the 1976 Act. I now turn to that issue.

Is Home Taping Fair Use?

The doctrine of fair use has been called, with some justification, "the most troublesome in the whole law of copyright." Although courts have constructed lists of factors to be considered in determining whether a particular use is fair, no fixed criteria have emerged by which that determination can be made. . . .

Despite this absence of clear standards, the fair use doctrine plays a crucial role in the law of copyright. The purpose of copyright protection, in the words of the Constitution, is to "promote the Progress of Science and useful Arts." Copyright is based on the belief that, by granting authors the exclusive rights to reproduce their works, they are given an incentive to create, and that "encouragement of individual effort by personal gain is the best way to advance public welfare through the talents of authors and inventors in 'science and the useful Arts.'" The monopoly created by copyright thus rewards the individual author in order to benefit the public.

There are situations, nevertheless, in which strict enforcement of this monopoly would inhibit the very "Progress of Science and useful Arts" that copyright is intended to promote. An obvious example is the researcher or scholar whose own work depends on the ability to refer to and to quote the work of prior scholars. Obviously, no author could create a new work if he were first required to repeat the research of every author who had gone before him. The scholar, like the ordinary user, of course could be left to bargain with each copyright owner for permission to quote from or refer to prior works. But there is a crucial difference between the scholar and the ordinary user. When the ordinary user decides that the owner's price is too high, and forgoes use of the work, only the individual is the loser. When the scholar forgoes the use of a prior work, not only does his own work suffer, but the public is deprived of his contribution to knowledge. The scholar's work, in other words, produces external benefits from which everyone profits. In such a case, the fair use doctrine acts as a form of subsidy—albeit at the first author's expense—to permit the second author to make limited use of the first author's work for the public good. Similar subsidy may be appropriate in a range of areas other than pure scholarship. The situations in which fair use is most commonly recognized are listed in [Section] 107 itself; fair use may be found when a work is used "for purposes such as criticism, comment, news reporting, teaching, . . . scholarship, or research." . . .

When a user reproduces an entire work and uses it for its original purpose, with no added benefit to the public, the doctrine of fair use usually does not apply. There is then no need whatsoever to provide the ordinary user with a fair use subsidy at the author's expense.

The making of a videotape recording for home viewing is an ordinary, rather than a productive, use of the Studios' copyrighted works. The District Court found that "Betamax owners use the copy for the same purpose as the original. They add nothing of their own." Although applying the fair use doctrine to home VTR recording, as Sony argues, may increase public access to material broadcast free over the public airwaves, I think Sony's argument misconceives the nature of copyright. Copyright gives the author a right to limit or even to cut off access to his work. A VTR recording creates no public benefit sufficient to justify limiting this right. Nor is this right extinguished by the copyright owner's choice to make the work available over the airwaves. Section 106 of the 1976 Act grants the copyright owner the exclusive right to control the performance and the reproduction of his work, and the fact that he has licensed a single television performance is really irrelevant to the existence of his right to control its reproduction. Although a television broadcast may be free to the viewer, this fact is equally irrelevant; a book borrowed from the public library may not be copied any more freely than a book that is purchased.

It may be tempting, as, in my view, the Court today is tempted, to stretch the doctrine of fair use so as to permit unfettered use of this new technology in order to increase access to television programming. But such an extension risks eroding the very basis of copyright law, by depriving authors of control over their works and consequently of their incentive to create. . . .

I recognize, nevertheless, that there are situations where permitting even an unproductive use would have no effect on the author's incentive to create, that is, where the use would not affect the value of, or the market for, the author's work. Photocopying an old newspaper clipping to send to a friend may be an example; pinning a quotation on one's bulletin board may be another. In each of these cases, the effect on the author is truly *de minimis* [unimportant]. Thus even though these uses provide no benefit to the public at large, no purpose is served by preserving the authors monopoly, and the use may be regarded as fair. . . .

Does Home Taping Affect the Market Value of Copyrighted Works?

At least when the proposed use is an unproductive one, a copyright owner need prove only a *potential* for harm to the market for or the value of the copyrighted work. Proof of actual harm, or even probable harm, may be impossible in an area where the effect of a new technology is speculative, and requiring such proof would present the "real danger . . . of confining the scope of an author's rights on the basis of the present technology so that, as the years go by, his copyright loses much of its value because of unforeseen technical advances." . . . Infringement thus would be found if the copyright owner demonstrates a reasonable possibility that harm will result from the proposed use. When the use is one that creates no benefit to the public at large, copyright protection should not be denied on the basis that a new technology that may result in harm has not yet done so.

The Studios have identified a number of ways in which VTR recording could damage their copyrights. VTR recording could reduce their ability to market their works in movie theaters and through the rental or sale of prerecorded videotapes or videodiscs; it also could reduce their rerun audience, and consequently the license fees available to them for repeated showings. Moreover, advertisers may be willing to pay for only "live" viewing audiences, if they believe VTR viewers will delete commercials or if rating services are unable to measure VTR use; if this is the case, VTR recording could reduce the license fees the Studios are able to charge even for first-run showings. Library-building may raise the potential for each of the types of harm identified by the Studios, and time-shifting may raise the potential for substantial harm as well. . . .

In this case, the Studios and their *amici* [friends of the court] demonstrate that the advent of the VTR technology created a potential market for their copyrighted programs. That market consists of those persons who find it impossible or inconvenient to watch the programs at the time they are broadcast, and who wish to watch them at other times. These persons are willing to pay for the privilege of watching copyrighted work at their convenience, as is evidenced by the fact that they are willing to pay for VTR's and tapes; undoubtedly, most also would be willing to pay some kind of royalty to copyright holders. The Studios correctly argue that they have been deprived of the ability to exploit this sizable market.

It is thus apparent from the record and from the findings of the District Court that time-shifting does have a substantial adverse effect upon the "potential market for" the Studios' copyrighted works. Accordingly, even under the formulation of the fair use doctrine advanced by Sony, time-shifting cannot be deemed a fair use.

Are VTR Manufacturers Liable for Copyright Infringement?

From the Studios' perspective, the consequences of home VTR recording are the same as if a business had taped the Studios' works off the air, duplicated the tapes, and sold or rented them to members of the public for home viewing. The distinction is that home VTR users do not record for commercial advantage; the commercial benefit accrues to the manufacturer and distributors of the Betamax. I thus must proceed to discuss whether the manufacturer and distributors can be held contributorily liable if the product they sell is used to infringe. . . .

In a case of this kind, . . . causation can be shown indirectly; it does not depend on evidence that particular Betamax owners relied on particular advertisements. . . .

The District Court found that Sony has advertised the Betamax as suitable for off-the-air recording of "favorite shows," "novels for television," and "classic movies," with no visible warning that such recording could constitute copyright infringement. It is only with the aid of the Betamax or some other VTR, that it is possible today for home television viewers to infringe copyright by recording off-the-air. Off-the-air recording is not only a foreseeable use for the Betamax, but indeed is its intended use. Under the circumstances, I agree with the Court of Appeals that, if off-the-air recording is an infringement of copyright, Sony has induced and materially contributed to the infringing conduct of Betamax owners.

Sony argues that the manufacturer or seller of a product used to infringe is absolved from liability whenever the product can be put to any substantial noninfringing use. . . .

As the District Court noted, if liability for contributory infringement were imposed on the manufacturer or seller of every product used to infringe—a typewriter, a camera, a photocopying machine—the "wheels of commerce" would be blocked.

I therefore conclude that, if a *significant* portion of the product's use is *noninfringing*, the manufacturers and sellers cannot be held contributorily liable for the product's infringing uses. If virtually all of the product's use, however, is to infringe, contributory liability may be imposed; if no one would buy the product for noninfringing purposes alone, it is clear that the manufacturer is purposely profiting from the infringement, and that liability is appropriately imposed. . . .

The key question is not the amount of television programming that is copyrighted, but rather the amount of VTR usage that is infringing. . . .

Is Home Taping for Time-Shifting a Copyright Infringement?

The Court's disposition of the case turns on its conclusion that time-shifting is a fair use. Because both parties agree that time-shifting is the primary use of VTR's, that conclusion, if correct, would settle the issue of Sony's liability under almost any definition of contributory infringement. The Court concludes that time-shifting is fair use for two reasons. Each is seriously flawed.

The Court's first reason for concluding that time-shifting is fair use is its claim that many copyright holders have no objection to time-shifting, and that "respondents have no right to prevent other copyright holders from authorizing it for their programs." The Court explains that a finding of contributory infringement would "inevitably frustrate the interests of broadcasters in reaching the portion of their audience that is available only through time-shifting."

Such reasoning, however, simply confuses the question of liability with the difficulty of fashioning an appropriate remedy. It may be that an injunction prohibiting the sale of VTR's would harm the interests of copyright holders who have no objection to others making copies of their programs. But such concerns should and would be taken into account in fashioning an appropriate remedy once liability has been found. Remedies may well be available that would not interfere with authorized time-shifting at all. The Court of Appeals mentioned the possibility of a royalty payment that would allow VTR sales and time-shifting to continue unabated, and the parties may be able to devise other narrowly tailored remedies. Sony may be able, for example, to build a VTR that enables broadcasters to scramble the signal of individual programs and "jam" the unauthorized recording of them. Even were an appropriate remedy not available at this time, the Court should not misconstrue copyright holders' rights in a manner that prevents enforcement of them when, through development of better techniques, an appropriate remedy becomes available.

The Court's second stated reason for finding that Sony is not liable for contributory infringement is its conclusion that even unauthorized time-shifting is fair use. This conclusion is even more troubling. The Court begins by suggesting that the fair use doctrine operates as a general "equitable rule of reason." That interpretation mischaracterizes the doctrine, and simply ignores the language of the statute. Section 107 establishes the fair use doctrine "for purposes such as criticism, comment, news reporting, teaching, . . . scholarship, or research." These are all productive uses. It is true that the legislative history states repeatedly that the doctrine must be applied flexibly on a case-by-case basis, but those references were only in the context of productive uses. Such a limitation on fair use comports with its purpose, which is to facilitate the creation of new works. There is no indication that the fair use doctrine has any application for purely personal consumption on the scale involved in this case. . . .

The Court confidently describes time-shifting as a non-commercial, nonprofit activity. It is clear, however, that personal use of programs that have been copied without permission is not what [Section] 107(1) protects. The intent of the section is to encourage users to engage in activities the primary benefit of which accrues to others. Time-shifting involves no such humanitarian impulse. It is likewise something of a mischaracterization of time-shifting to describe it as non-commercial in the sense that that term is used in the statute. As one commentator has observed, time-shifting is noncommercial in the same sense that stealing jewelry and wearing it—instead of reselling it—is noncommercial. Purely consumptive uses are certainly not what the fair use doctrine was designed to protect. . . .

Time-Shifting Does Not Qualify as Fair Use

The third statutory factor—"the amount and substantiality of the portion used"—is even more devastating to the Court's interpretation. It is undisputed that virtually all VTR owners record entire works, thereby creating an exact substitute for the copyrighted original. Fair use is intended to allow individuals engaged in productive uses to copy small portions of original works that will facilitate their own productive endeavors. Time-shifting bears no resemblance to such activity, and the complete duplication that it involves might alone be sufficient to preclude a finding of fair use. It is little wonder that the Court has chosen to ignore this statutory factor.

The fourth factor requires an evaluation of "the effect of the use upon the potential market for or value of the copyrighted work." This is the factor upon which the Court focuses, but once again, the Court has misread the statute. As mentioned above, the statute requires a court to consider the effect of the use on the *potential* market for the copyrighted work. The Court has struggled mightily to show that VTR use has not *reduced* the value of the Studios' copyrighted works in their *present* markets. Even if true, that showing only begins the proper inquiry. The development of the VTR has created a new market for the works produced by the Studios. That market consists of those persons who desire to view television programs at times other than when they are broadcast, and who therefore purchase VTR recorders to enable them to time-shift. Because time-shifting of the Studios' copyrighted works involves the copying of them, however, the Studios are entitled to share in the benefits of that new market. Those benefits currently go to Sony through Betamax sales. Respondents therefore can show harm from VTR use simply by showing that the value of their copyrights would increase if they were compensated for the copies that are used in the new market. The existence of this effect is self-evident. . . .

The Court explains that a manufacturer of a product is not liable for contributory infringement as long as the product is "*capable* of substantial noninfringing uses." Such a definition essentially eviscerates the concept of contributory infringement. Only the most unimaginative manufacturer would be unable to demonstrate that a image-duplicating product is "capable" of substantial noninfringing uses. Surely Congress desired to prevent the sale of products that are used almost exclusively to infringe copyrights; the fact that noninfringing uses exist presumably would have little bearing on that desire. . . .

Like so many other problems created by the interaction of copyright law with a new technology, "[t]here can be no really satisfactory solution to the problem presented here, until Congress acts." But in the absence of a congressional solution, courts cannot avoid difficult problems by refusing to apply the law. We must "take the Copyright Act . . . as we find it" and "do as little damage as possible to traditional copyright principles . . . until the Congress legislates."

> *"The home-counterfeiting of copyrighted plays, novels or films is no more justifiable because it is done at home and for the home-owner's sole benefit than would be the home-counterfeiting of $10 bills."*

Home Taping of Television Shows Is Not Fair Use

Irwin Karp

Irwin Karp was the attorney for the Authors League of America. The following viewpoint is the brief he wrote for the Supreme Court representing the Authors League as amicus curiae (friend of the court) in Sony v. Universal Studios. *In it he argues that home recording of television programs does not fall under the "fair use" provision of the copyright law, which was not intended to cover entire films or plays, and that allowing it would be harmful to authors. It would be no different from distribution of copyrighted works by pirates, he says, because the end result would be to place copyrighted works permanently into the hands of thousands of individual viewers without any compensation to authors. It would diminish the market for authorized commercial copies of such works, he says, and would prevent programs from being rerun. Furthermore, in the opinion of the Authors League, it would discourage the production of worthwhile new programs that cannot make a profit on their initial presentation, since there would be no aftermarket for them.*

Irwin Karp, brief of the Authors League of America as amicus curiae, *Sony Corporation of America v. Universal City Studios and Walt Disney Productions*, October 21, 1982.

The Authors League of America is the national society of professional authors and dramatists. One of its principal purposes is to express the views of its 11,000 members in cases involving the rights of authors under the United States Copyright Act.

The League files this brief (with the parties' consent) because this appeal raises questions of enormous importance and grave concern to authors and dramatists. The Court of Appeals decision correctly decided that home-recording of broadcast motion pictures and television programs infringed rights granted under [Section] 106 of the Copyright Act. Reversal of that decision would destroy or greatly erode the rights of novelists and playrights, as well as those of motion picture companies and television producers, and seriously impede the production and distribution of literary and dramatic works, and of films and television programs based upon them.

The Authors League agrees completely with the opinion and conclusions of the Court of Appeals, and we will not burden the Court with a prolonged reiteration of the analysis and authorities set out in its opinion. We do wish to discuss the consequences of the decision, or its reversal, for authors and playwrights.

The Effect of Home-Recording on Authors' Rights

Sec. 106 of the Copyright Act grants authors—writers and dramatists as well as motion picture producers—the "exclusive right(s) to reproduce (their) copyrighted works in copies or phonorecords." The Section does not limit the right of reproduction by the condition that it be "public", as is the case with the rights of performance and display. Nor do any of the specific limitations on the right of reproduction, in Secs. 110, 112, 115 and 118, permit unauthorized home-recording of broadcast motion pictures or television programs. Clearly, such home-recording violated the rights of the motion picture producer-respondents in this case, as it would violate the rights of a dramatist whose play was televised or transmitted by cable (an increasingly-popular means of presenting "live" stage performances to home audiences).

Modern technology, moreover, makes it impossible to draw any meaningful copyright distinction between reproduction of a copyrighted film or play, in cassettes, by a commercial pirate or by individuals in their homes. If a commercial pirate reproduced 10 videocassettes of Stephen Sondheim's acclaimed musical play *Sweeney Todd* by taping the recent cable transmission of a stage performance, in his home, that would be an infringement of copyright under Sec. 106(1). It would be no less an infringement because the pirate distributed the copies, one to a customer, to 10 individuals for use in their homes. The essence of most infringements of the right of reproduction is the making of copies for distribution to ultimate consumers for use in their homes.

Furthermore, it makes no difference whether the piracy is undertaken for profit or for not-for-profit. If a school taped the *Sweeney Todd* performance and distributed 10 copies to students without charge for use at home, it would violate the author's copyright.

The modern technology of the Betamax and other home video-recording machines makes it possible for 10, or 1,000 or 1,000,000 individuals to by-pass the commercial pirate and reproduce video-cassettes of *Sweeney Todd* or a Disney movie from a single television or cable broadcast. For the author, the copyright and economic consequences are the same as those of commercial piracy: 10, or 1,000 or 1,000,000 copies have been reproduced and placed in the possession of individuals—who make up the author's audience—without his/her permission and without any compensation. The home-counterfeiting of copyrighted plays, novels or films is no more justifiable because it is done at home and for the home-owner's sole benefit than would be the home-counterfeiting of

$10 bills, performed on a sophisticated copying-machine equivalent of the Betamax for the benefit and enjoyment of the home-owner.

The Court of Appeals correctly ruled that home-recording of copyrighted works is not fair use. As it noted, the doctrine of fair use was not intended to permit the reproduction of entire works to satisfy the very purposes for which authors license the production and distribution of copies, and the broadcast and presentation of performances: to entertain individual readers and listeners.

The accumulation of home-recorded copies of a broadcast or cable transmission of a play, film or television program cannot satisfy the tests of fair use in Sec. 107, and particularly cannot survive the test of "the effect of the use upon the potential market for or value of the copyrighted work."

The Economic Effect of Home-Recording on Authors

The accumulation of home-recordings of a performance of *Sweeney Todd* or other plays or musicals has an adverse and pervasive effect on potential markets for that dramatic work, as it does on the potential market for any motion picture which is reproduced, by home-recording, in countless video-cassettes. Obviously, home-recording displaces the sales of commercially-produced cassettes licensed by the author or film company, and deprives those copyright owners of income from such sales.

Beyond that, however, home-recording diminishes many potential markets for films and plays. The broadcast which provided the means of counterfeiting was intended to be ephemeral, as it was prior to the perfection of affordable home-recording machines. An ephemeral presentation of any work—by broadcast, on the stage, or in motion picture theatre—does not exhaust the work's appeal to the audiences that view it. Countless movie-goers see the same film many times; television viewers, by the millions, watch re-runs of their favorite programs; theatre-goers will see revivals of their favorite plays in first-class, regional, stock and amateur performances, or in motion picture adaptations.

But thousands or hundreds of thousands of home-recordings of a play or film will have an enormous adverse effect on these potential markets for dramatic and literary works. They will prevent many plays, films and television programs from being revived, rerun or rebroadcast; and, in a vast number of instances, will reduce sharply the number of subsequent presentations in various media. All of this, without providing authors and producers income from the source which diminished their potential markets ... the unauthorized home-recordings of their copyrighted works.

The authors of plays and musical plays, who license performance, recording and broadcast rights in their works, will be directly injured. If they authorize a cable transmission of their plays, home-recording threatens them with serious loss of income from stock, amateur, regional and other theatrical productions of their works. Yet the granting of cable-transmission rights is an important means of raising funds to produce plays in a theater whose costs have escalated far beyond the rate of inflation.

Many authors who write films and television programs will be injured since a portion of their compensation is a share of the proceeds or profits derived by the motion picture or television producer from television and cable broadcasts of the works they write. Similarly, many authors of books and plays, who sell the motion picture or television rights in their works, will be injured since their compensation often is based, in part, on the income derived from the company which produced the film or television program based on their writings.

The Effect of Home-Recording on Program Production

Another wide spread consequence of unauthorized and uncompensated home-recording of broadcast motion pictures, plays and television programs may well be the drying-up of financing for worthwhile films and television programs. While the few commercial blockbusters each year may be able to earn huge profits on their initial theatrical exhibition, this is not true of many films and programs that have significant dramatic, cultural or social value. Many of these do not recoup their costs of production from theatrical exhibition or network broadcasting. They must have access to all of the after-markets to repay their investors and to earn reasonable profits for the authors and producers who risked years of work, talent and capital to create them. The term "fair use" cannot, by any stretch of imagination or casuistry, be applied to the unauthorized recording of a production embodying the diverse talents, creative efforts and financial investment of authors, directors, actors, designers, cinematographers and many others.

It is obvious that Congress did not exclude home-recording from the reach of the author's exclusive right of reproduction. It is equally obvious that Congress will enact some "solution" to the home-recording problem if this Court affirms the Court of Appeals' decision. The public will have no dearth of champions in Congress to protect its interests. And it is likely that Congress will enact some method of compulsory licensing and payment to compensate authors and motion picture producers for the serious loss of income they will suffer from continued home-recording.

But if the Court were to reverse the Court of Appeals decision, authors and motion picture companies will be under a severe handicap in obtaining legislation that will provide reasonable compensation for the reproduction of their works by home recorders, and for the substantial loss of potential markets and of value of their works home-recording will increasingly cause.

The solution is one that Congress should enact. It is far less likely to be equitable if the Court does not follow the clear meaning of the Copyright Act and affirm the Court of Appeals' decision.

> "An affirmance [of the lower court's rul-
> ing] by the Court ... would make mil-
> lions of Americans into lawbreakers."

The Supreme Court Debated Home Taping of Television Shows at Length

Jonathan Band and Andrew J. McLaughlin

*Jonathan Band is an attorney specializing in intellectual prop-
erty law. At the time the following article was written, Andrew J.
McLaughlin was a student at Harvard Law School. In the article, they tell what the papers of Justice Thurgood Marshall—
made public after his death—reveal about the debate in the Supreme Court over the case of* Sony v. Universal Studios. *The
circuit court had ruled that home videotaping of television programs was a violation of copyright law and that Sony was also
liable because it was aware that its Betamax VCRs (then called
VTRs) would be used for illegal taping. The justices of the Supreme Court were divided in their opinions about the case and
discussed it among themselves for a whole year. For a majority
Supreme Court opinion to be issued, at least five justices must
agree enough with what it says to sign their names to it. In this
case, it initially appeared that the majority thought the circuit
court's ruling should be upheld, but as the argument progressed,
those holding to that position became the minority, and the
original majority opinion, written by Justice Harry Blackmun,
became the dissenting one. The circuit court was overruled by a*

vote of five to four. If it had not been, VCRs might have become illegal to sell in the United States and the video rental industry might never have developed.

Justice [Thurgood] Marshall's files reveal that four justices—[Warren] Burger, [John Paul] Stevens, [Sandra Day] O'Connor, and [Harry] Blackmun—voted in favor of granting Sony's petition for writ of certiorari [review], while the other five justices opposed the petition. Of the four supporting the petition, only Justice Blackmun ultimately sought to affirm the Ninth Circuit's ruling that private non-commercial home videotaping of copyrighted television broadcasts constituted an infringement, and accordingly that Sony and its co-defendants were liable for contributory infringement. Thus, had Justice Blackmun *opposed* the petition, it would not have been granted, and the Ninth Circuit's holding would have remained intact. Although Justice Blackmun probably supported the petition because he thought that the Supreme Court would affirm the Ninth Circuit, it proved to be a dangerous strategy.

After oral argument on January 18, 1983, the tentative vote in the January 21 conference had Justices Marshall, Blackmun, [Lewis] Powell, and [William] Rehnquist voting to affirm the Ninth Circuit. The other justices either voted to reverse the Ninth Circuit, or expressed only tentative positions, apparently giving Justice Marshall's group the best chance to form a majority. The senior justice in the apparent majority, Justice Marshall, informed Chief Justice Burger that he had assigned the opinion affirming the Ninth Circuit to Justice Blackmun.

On January 24, 1983, Justice Stevens sent a letter to Justice Blackmun, to which he attached a memorandum that he had dictated for his own use four days earlier. Justice Stevens, who supported reversal of the Ninth Circuit opinion, wrote to outline "the point that most strongly supports a reversal" which he believed had been inadequately developed at oral argument. . . .

The central question for Justice Stevens was whether the making of a single copy of any copyrighted work for a private, noncommercial use is a copyright infringement. Stevens noted that legislative debate in 1971 favored allowing home taping of sound recordings. Further, although Congress was aware of the practice of private copying of sound recordings, [Section] 106 of the 1976 Copyright Act contains "no prohibition against the reproduction of a single copy for the private use of the person making the reproduction." Stevens argued that in light of Congress' deliberate refusal to confront the issue of private copying when it revised the statute, courts must consider three "values" pointing in the direction of finding the practice lawful: (1) privacy interests, (2) the principle of fair warning to millions of home copiers, and (3) the economic interest in not imposing substantial retroactive fines on an entrepreneur who has successfully developed a new and useful product, "particularly when the evidence as found by the district court indicates that the copyright holders have not yet suffered any actual harm."

An affirmance by the Court, Justice Stevens added, would make millions of Americans into lawbreakers, liable to copyright holders for statutory damages of $100 per copy. Justice Stevens wrote that "[w]e would hardly encourage respect for the law if we were to announce in effect: 'Anyone who time shifts a single copy of a sportscast owes the copyright holder either $250 or $100, but fear not because this law will never be enforced.'" . . .

Opposing Drafts of Blackmun and Stevens

The first draft of Justice Blackmun's opinion for the majority was circulated to the Court on June 13, 1983. The draft opinion bore strong resemblance to Justice Blackmun's eventual dissent. After reciting the facts of the case and providing a brief overview of the exclusive rights granted by the Copyright Act, Justice Blackmun painstakingly refuted Justice

Stevens' (and the district court's) private copying argument. Justice Blackmun then turned to Section 107, stressing that for a use to be fair, it usually must be productive. Justice Blackmun acknowledged that unproductive uses could be fair, but only if they caused *de minimis* [minimal] harm. In such cases, he shifted the burden of proof to the defendants: "when the proposed use is an unproductive one, a copyright owner need produce only evidence of a potential for harm. Infringement then will be found, unless the user can demonstrate affirmatively that permitting the use would have no tendency to harm the market for or the value of the copyrighted work." Justice Blackmun proceeded to overturn the district court's finding that the studios had suffered no harm. He next analyzed contributory infringement. Justice Blackmun argued that a manufacturer of a product whose "most conspicuous purpose" was infringement should be liable for contributory infringement. Because the district court had made no finding on the proportion of VTR (videotape recorder) recording that was infringing, Justice Blackmun ordered a remand for further consideration of this issue. He also ordered a remand on remedies, suggesting that the district court consider imposing royalties on the sale of VTRs.

Meanwhile, perhaps sensing that at least one member of the tentative majority could be persuaded to join him, Justice Stevens circulated a draft opinion. . . . Justice Stevens' draft addressed only the issue of private copying, reiterating the argument, made first in his letter of January 24, that Congress had not prohibited it under the 1976 Act. . . .

Justice Stevens' follow-up memorandum, circulated later that day (June 13, 1983), cited broad underlying areas of agreement between Justice Blackmun's opinion and his own, and limited disagreement to the question of how the Court should resolve an issue which Congress knowingly failed to address: in this case, private copying. Justice Stevens understood the 1971 House Report to suggest that noncommercial home taping was exempt, and he interpreted the explicit "fair use" exemptions of the 1976 Act not to alter the rules on private home recording. . . .

Justices Blackmun and Stevens also differed over the social value of the practice of time shifting. While Justice Blackmun found that "VTR recording creates no public benefits sufficient to justify [allowing it]," Justice Stevens argued that "time shifting makes television programming available to viewers who would otherwise miss it," thus serving a public interest.

Justice Blackmun responded to Justice Stevens' criticisms on June 14, 1983, with a memorandum to the Conference. In response to Justice Stevens' position that Congress ought to take the lead in responding to new technologies, Justice Blackmun asserted that Congress had done so only because the Court's response in the past to new technologies had been to construe copyright law narrowly, provoking Congressional reaction. Justice Blackmun believed that unlike previous copyright laws, the 1976 Act was intended to cover all technologies and uses, "whether or not they were specifically contemplated or even known at the time the Act was passed." . . .

Brennan's Third Alternative

Also on June 14, 1983, Justice [William] Brennan joined the debate "with some trepidation," and placed on the table a "third alternative." At Conference, Justice Brennan had supported a partial affirmance of the Ninth Circuit, drawing a distinction within fair use doctrine between "time-shifting" (fair use) and "library building" (infringement). Justice Brennan now wrote that he agreed with Justice Stevens that the lower court should be overruled outright. He added, however, that he

> cannot agree with [Stevens] that Congress has implicitly enacted a broad exemption from the Copyright Act for all cases of private, noncommercial, single-copy reproduction. . . . The home-use audio exemption, if it ex-

ists, was the product of a specific political compromise, and it cannot provide a theoretical basis for a broader exemption.

Justice Brennan endorsed Justice Blackmun's reasoning that "Sony can be liable for contributory infringement only if the Betamax's 'most conspicuous purpose' or 'primary use' is an infringing use." Justice Brennan, however, believed "that a good deal of timeshifting is fair use." He further believed that the studio's allegations of potential harm "are simply empty when applied to most timeshifting." Accordingly, Justice Brennan could not "agree that the Betamax's 'primary use' is infringement" nor "that the Copyright Act authorizes the sort of complex, multiparty proceeding that Harry [Blackmun]'s opinion contemplates to frame an appropriate remedy." ...

Justice White's Compromise

On June 17, 1983, Justice [Byron] White attempted to broker a compromise between the Stevens and Brennan approaches. Justice White was not convinced that Congress either before or after the 1976 Act "intended each home recorder of copyrighted works to be an infringer, whether he records sound or video." Justice White felt that, before 1976, the home recorder clearly did not infringe, and that Congress did not intend to change the law in that respect in 1976: "Thus I cannot agree with Harry [Blackmun]'s draft and am closer to John [Stevens] than to you [Brennan]." Nevertheless, given that no relief was sought against the homeowner and that both Justices Brennan and Stevens agreed that Sony was not a contributory infringer, albeit for different reasons, Justice White asked, "Need the status of the homeowner be decided at all?" Driving his point home, Justice White said, "If there were five votes to reverse as to Sony, the issue of the homeowner is hardly a pressing question." Justice White appeared to be suggesting that so long as some uses of the VTR are legitimate (*e.g.*, time shifting), Sony is not a contributory infringer, and thus the Court simply need not reach the issue of whether the homeowner's other possible uses of the VTR (*e.g.*, library building) infringe.

Justice Stevens wrote back to Justice White, agreeing to his compromise solution and offering to recast his opinion if five votes could be won by avoiding the issue of the homeowner's status. . . .

Justice Blackmun . . . stressed that "most Betamax owners would not have bought the device if they were restricted to noninfringing uses." However, Justice Blackmun again compromised:

> I am willing, however, to adopt Sandra [O'Connor]'s proposed standard for contributory infringement, provided that an opinion for the Court can thereby be obtained. I agree that the question of contributory infringement turns on the amount of VTR use that is infringing rather than the amount of television programming that is copyrighted.

Justice Blackmun concluded by noting that Justices Marshall and Rehnquist had yet to indicate their agreement with the changes. . . .

Justice O'Connor wanted to stress that "contributory infringement may result from either inducement or material contribution." She proposed to "accept the district court's finding that Sony did not induce any infringement." Moreover, she differed with Justice Blackmun over the import of [previous] cases "because they involved instances of *control* by the party found to be the contributory infringer. Whatever else the VTR manufacturers may do, they certainly do not have any control over VTR users." For Justice O'Connor the proper standard was: "is the VTR *capable* of substantial noninfringing uses?" Justice O'Connor proposed that Justice Blackmun alter his opinion to read as follows:

> We therefore conclude that there can be no contributory infringement if the VTR is capable of significant noninfringing uses. If a significant portion of what is available to copy

on the VTR is either not copyrightable or is copyrighted but the owners have authorized copying, then the VTR must be deemed capable of substantial noninfringing uses irrespective of the actual uses to which VTR's are put.

Justice O'Connor indicated that she would join Justice Blackmun's opinion if he made her changes. This letter clearly reflects the evolution of Justice O'Connor's thinking since her first memorandum to Justice Blackmun five days earlier. Then, she wrote that "the 'fair use' exemption is not applicable in this case." Now, she believed that timeshifting could be fair use, and accordingly, that Sony was not a contributory infringer. . . .

In the June 27 draft Justice Stevens completed the discussion of the other factors compelling a conclusion of fair use. He conceded that the legislative history of the 1976 Act does not expressly focus on the question of time-shifting, but proceeds to devote nearly six pages to "two clues that strongly support the conclusion that Congress assumed that such private use was entirely legitimate." Justice Stevens then examined policy reasons supporting a fair use finding, notably "[s]pecial constitutional values . . . implicated whenever the Government seeks to regulate or prohibit conduct that take [sic] place entirely within the privacy of the home." This policy discussion derives from Justice Stevens' earlier draft favoring a private copying exemption. The next day, June 28, Justice Stevens circulated yet another draft of his opinion. Substantively the same as the June 27 draft, the new draft included lengthy references to the record in the sections treating authorized time shifting and market impact. The June 28 draft omitted several passages in the June 27 draft, including the suggestion that Section 106 could be read to exempt private copying. Thus, in the June 28 draft Justice Stevens' private copying argument disappeared for good.

Justice Blackmun's Line in the Sand

Also on June 28, while Justice Stevens was circulating his latest draft, Justice Blackmun responded to Justice O'Connor, refusing to make the changes recommended in her June 21 letter. Justice Blackmun declared that "[f]ive votes are not that important to me when I feel that proper legal principles are involved. It therefore looks as though you and I are in substantial disagreement. The case will have to go its own way by a different route from the one I have proposed."

Rejected by Justice Blackmun, Justice O'Connor turned to the Stevens opinion, which had already been endorsed by Justice Brennan. Justice O'Connor wrote to Chief Justice Burger that after "many late nights, and much redrafting . . . [t]he result has been a decided shift to a 'middle' position on the merits and a movement toward a more restrictive stance on contributory infringement." Since Justice Blackmun refused to make any further changes to his approach, Justice O'Connor stated that she was closer to Justice Stevens' opinion than to any other "on the table." . . .

Justice Marshall wrote to Justice Blackmun on June 28, saying simply "I am still with you." Justice White stated that while he preferred Justice Stevens' opinion to any others, the case ought to be held over to be reargued the next term: "I would feel more comfortable if we could give the case more attention than time will now allow." Justice Rehnquist wrote a memorandum to the conference endorsing White's suggestion. The next day, the Conference decided without further written communication to hold the case over for reargument in the fall.

Reargument occurred on October 3, 1983. The next day, Justice Marshall circulated a letter addressing "the economic impact of time-shifting on copyright holders." Justice Marshall argued that the criterion of impact on potential markets stated in [Section] 107 of the 1976 Copyright Act has two implications. First, an infringer cannot prevail merely by demonstrating that the copyright holder suffered no net harm from the infringer's actions. . . . Rather, the infringer must demonstrate that he has not impaired the copyright holder's ability to demand compensation from (or to deny access to) any group of people who would otherwise be willing to pay to scc or hear the copyrighted work.

Second, "the fact that a given market for a copyrighted work would not be available to the copyright holder were it not for the infringer's activities does not permit the infringer to exploit that market without compensating the copyright holder."

Justice Marshall argued that though VTR manufacturers may have created a new market for movie studios' copyrighted works (people unable to watch the programs when broadcast), the studios have nevertheless "been deprived of the ability to exploit this sizeable market." He also suggested that most of these viewers "would also be willing to pay some kind of royalty to the copyright holders." To Sony's argument that time-shifters compensate the Studios in exactly the same manner as "live" viewers by watching the advertisements, Justice Marshall responded that there was no evidence that rating services measured or would measure time-shifters to estimate the audience size for which the Studios were compensated. He also pointed out that sizeable numbers of time-shifters edit out the advertisements.

Thus, Justice Marshall concluded, "time-shifting cannot be deemed a fair user," because "time-shifting does have a substantial adverse effect upon 'the potential market for' [the Studios'] copyrighted works." While recognizing that his argument was not dispositive of the case, "the decision below can be reversed only if a sufficient amount of home VTR taping is 'unchallenged' by the owners of the copyrights on the programs being copied to enable Sony to satisfy whatever test for contributory infringement the Court settles upon." . . .

What If the Court Had Decided Differently?

The Marshall papers reflect the significant contributions made by Justices Brennan, White and O'Connor to the Stevens opinion. Although Stevens was initially prepared to reverse the Ninth Circuit on the grounds that private copying did not infringe any of the exclusive rights granted by copyright, Justices Brennan and White convinced him to base the reversal on fair use and contributory infringement. The standard for contributory infringement—that liability would not attach if the equipment was capable of substantial noninfringing uses—derives from Justices Brennan and O'Connor. The fair use analysis—such as it is—also derives from Justices Brennan and O'Connor. . . .

The Marshall papers reveal the evolution of Justice Blackmun's dissent from his draft majority opinion. The dissent includes a discussion, taken from Justice Marshall's Memorandum of October 4, on the effect of VTR recording on the potential market for the studio's works. The dissent also reflects Justice O'Connor's suggestions, including: diluting the "most conspicuous purpose" standard for contributory infringement; removing from the defendant the burden of proving the absence of harm; and eliminating the outright reversal of the District Court's findings on harm. Justice Blackmun's dissent also contains a new Section VI criticizing the majority's fair use analysis. . . .

The Marshall papers provide copyright lawyers with the opportunity to play the favorite game of historians: "What If?" What if Blackmun had voted against the petition for certiorari, or if a majority had joined Justice Blackmun in finding the home taping of television broadcasts [not] to be a fair use? On remand, the District Court may have eliminated the VTR from the U.S. market. This may have precluded the development of the video rental industry, the source both of significant revenues to the studios and of empowerment to consumers who can now choose their own television programming. If the District Court had pursued this remedy, Congress may have responded with a compulsory license scheme similar to the 1992 digital audio recording legislation. Alternatively, the District Court may have imposed its own compulsory licensing regime on VTRs.

And what if Stevens' private copying rationale had prevailed? Congress may have amended the Copyright Act to expressly prohibit private copying, or it may have enacted compulsory licensing regimes for technologies which facilitate copying. Then again, Congress may have done nothing, implicitly agreeing with the Court that the 1976 Copyright Act did not prohibit private copying.

In the end, however, none of these things happened. The Court rejected both the Blackmun and Stevens extremes, and found a middle ground from which our current fair use jurisprudence has blossomed.

"We will not have creative and original works of art—such as television shows and movies worthy of copying—unless those investing in them can ensure a return on their investment."

The Precedent Set by *Sony v. Universal* Has Resulted in Illegal Downloading

Marci Hamilton

Marci Hamilton is a professor at the Benjamin N. Cardozo School of Law, Yeshiva University, in New York City, and is an internationally recognized expert on constitutional and copyright law. She is the author of several books. In the following viewpoint she discusses Internet sites that infringe copyrights by linking to other sites in countries that do not enforce copyright laws. In her opinion, the Supreme Court's decision in Sony v. Universal Studios *paved the way for this practice by holding that Sony was not liable for copyright violations committed by people who used the VCRs it manufactured. The Court did not realize, she says, that users would make libraries of shows instead of merely time-shifting. She feels that this decision should be reversed, or at least clarified, to make plain that facilitating the illegal downloading of copies over the Internet is a copyright infringement. She argues that sites doing this should be shut down, but since enforcement is difficult and expensive, the television and motion picture industries should be encouraged to find technological means of preventing such downloading.*

Marci Hamilton, "It's Time for the Supreme Court's Sony Betamax Decision to Be Reversed," *Findlaw.com*, April 19, 2007. Reproduced by permission. http://writ.new.findlaw.com/hamilton/20070419.html

The Wall Street Journal's front page [on April 17, 2007,] reported on the new practice of creating "guerrilla video sites"—websites that offer menus of links to illegal video copies of television shows and movies.

For obvious reasons, the television and motion picture industries are not happy with the sites. For equally obvious reasons, the practice of posting the links is illegal: a prime example of contributory copyright infringement.

In this column, I will explain one of the leading influences on the creation of such sites: The Supreme Court's 1984 decision in the *Sony* [*v. Universal Studios*] case, which gave the Court's blessing to the use of VCRs. Then, twenty-three years ago, the Court—understandably—did not foresee how copies would be made, used, and stored in the future; as a result, it set a precedent that is encouraging contributory infringers to believe that they might not actually be infringing copyright.

No Justified Defense

If one ever lacked a reminder of the greediness of human nature, a few minutes on the Internet would make the point impossible to forget. The list of entities willing (at some point) to use the Internet to get for free what they should have purchased is long.

Originally, Napster was their poster boy, but now we have high school dropouts "pioneering" a new way to steal content, on their guerrilla sites, by simply linking to content on sites whose servers are located in places like China—which is not known for its copyright enforcement, to put it mildly.

These "guerrilla" sites are obviously violating copyright law, though their "defense" is that the illegal material is not on their site. Can there be any doubt that they are committing contributory copyright infringement, when the entire purpose for the site is to ceaselessly compile and collect links to available illegal material? Indeed, if their "customers" complain about the quality of a link, they search assiduously for a better one—to make their users' copyright-infringing viewing even more pleasant.

Those who may be foolish enough to advertise on these sites should beware as well: Their dollars are also contributing to the business of contributory copyright infringement.

As with the original incarnation of Napster, the problem here is not only with the service, but also with those all too willing to enjoy the illegal materials. If every citizen who would never dream of stealing groceries from a supermarket, would also refuse to steal television shows and movies, then the guerrilla site operators would largely be entertaining themselves. Unfortunately, it is taking longer than it should for even otherwise upstanding citizens to decide to stay solely on the legal side of the copyright line.

It took lawsuits and threats to universities to bring file-sharing sites like the early Napster somewhat under control, and it will doubtless take similar measures here. No doubt, these measures will be at least somewhat effective: Once any potential advertisers understand the illegal nature of the service they are supporting, and their own possible legal exposure, they are likely to take their dollars elsewhere.

On the other hand, users may still end up being directly charged—or voluntarily paying to keep the sites afloat, as sometimes occurs with popular blogs. In addition, the site creators may continue to work onward for the sheer thrill of lawbreaking and prestige within their communities.

A Crucial Error

As noted above, the Supreme Court's 1984 decision in *Sony* paved the way, in a sense, for sites like these. There, the Court held that Betamax was not liable for copyright infringement for copies made by their machines of television shows, because its product was used solely for "time-shifting" television viewing—a "substantial noninfringing use"—and not for librarying the materials. On this rationale, the Court found the copying to be "fair use," despite the fact that entire shows were copied. Time does, however, test decisions, and this one should be overruled—or, at a minimum, updated to clarify that current VCR-like practices on the Internet are nevertheless contributory copyright infringements.

Consider, for example, one key basis for the *Sony* holding that is utterly absent with respect to the guerrilla sites: The *Sony* Court held that there was a significant likelihood that the copyright holders licensing their work for broadcast television would not object to the copying for the purpose of time-shifting. This was a strange point even at the time: Who did the Court think was complaining about the copying? Now, the copyright holders' objections to infringement, including to guerrilla sites, are deafening.

Another key basis for the *Sony* holding is also lacking today. There, the Court found no likelihood of harm to a potential market: In its eyes, it didn't and shouldn't matter to advertisers and copyright holders whether VCR users watched a show the moment it aired, or a few hours later.

Even then, the existence of users who "libraried" tapes made this argument questionable. Today, the argument is demonstrably entirely wrong: Users frequently do library what they download, not to mention make additional copies for others, and copyright infringement can drain profits that should go to the copyright user. In addition to television shows, as noted above, guerrilla sites typically link to pirated (often lower-quality) copies of movies their users would otherwise pay to watch in the theater or on DVD. The copyright infringement is twofold: first, for the illegal copying, and second, for creating a derivative work that misrepresents the original work being pirated.

Aggressive Action Should Be Taken

In sum, the video guerillas are engaging in blatant contributory infringement—and that justifies shutting down their sites. But how? When one site closes, another may open soon after. Enforcement remains very expensive for the copyright owners—and that is a serious problem.

There is, however, at least a silver lining here. It is in everyone's interest to encourage the wealthy television and motion picture industries to research technological means of setting up effective "fences" and "alarms" on the Internet. Instead of chasing infringers, we need better means of preventing poaching in the first place.

After all, we will not have creative and original works of art—such as television shows and movies worthy of copying—unless those investing in them can ensure a return on their investment. Moreover, "fences," "alarms," and tracking devices have important side-benefits, too: They can be used to protect our children, prevent predation or catch predators, and shut down child-accessible pornography sites. The copyright industry has an opportunity here to protect its own wealth, which is the American way, but in so doing, it can also contribute to the greater safety of every American.

As it is, we remain in an Internet limbo, no longer in the Wild West but still with inadequate "fences" and "alarms."

To protect the quality of American creative works, we need to ensure the copyright laws are enforced against those, like the video guerillas, who shamelessly piggyback on others' contributions to society.

CHAPTER 2

News Media
May Not Use
Unpublished Material
Without Permission

Case Overview

Harper & Row, Publishers, Inc. v. Nation Enterprises (1985)

In 1979, former U.S. president Gerald Ford finished writing his memoirs, having previously signed a contract with Harper & Row for them to be published as a book titled *A Time to Heal.* The contract gave Harper & Row ownership of the copyright, including the right to license the publication of excerpts from the memoirs prior to the book's appearance. *Time* magazine made an agreement with Harper & Row that allowed it to print 7,500 words of the text in exchange for $25,000, half of which was paid in advance.

Shortly before the *Time* article was to appear, another magazine, *The Nation,* got hold of a copy of the unpublished book manuscript. An editor of *The Nation* wrote a 2,250-word article that included about 300 words of direct quotations taken from that manuscript without permission. It was timed to "scoop" the *Time* article. Because of this, *Time* canceled its article and refused to pay the remaining $12,500 to Harper & Row, as their agreement permitted it to do if any of the material became public prematurely. Harper & Row then sued *The Nation* for violation of the Copyright Act.

The district court held that the Ford memoirs were protected by copyright and that *The Nation*'s article was an infringement. *The Nation* was ordered to pay Harper & Row the money it had lost by the cancellation of the agreement with *Time.* The Court of Appeals, however, reversed this decision, ruling that the inclusion of quotations in *The Nation* was "fair use," which is allowed under the Copyright Act for purposes such as commentary and news reporting. Harper & Row maintained that it was not a fair use because it led to the loss of money and because the author's right to choose when and where to make the text public had not been honored. It was up to the Supreme Court to decide which view would prevail.

The book excerpts in *The Nation*'s article were not large, and they did not constitute a continuous block of text—there were only scattered sentences here and there, arranged in an order different from the way they appeared in the book. But they were important excerpts. They dealt with President Ford's recollections of the Watergate crisis that had led to the resignation of President Richard Nixon and Ford's subsequent pardon of Nixon. They included details not previously revealed to the public, and were therefore newsworthy. On one hand, the fact that they were such a significant part of the book gave Ford's right to control their release more weight than it would otherwise have received. On the other hand, some members of the Court believed that the excerpts' news value gave the public a right to see them as soon as possible. They felt that the disputed passages consisted mainly of ideas and information, which cannot be copyrighted, rather than an author's unique expression of those ideas. The purpose of copyright, they said, is to encourage the dissemination of information, and calling the immediate publication of newsworthy information unfair is contrary to that purpose.

The Court ruled six to three in favor of Harper & Row. The right of first publication normally outweighs a claim of fair use, said the majority, and that right—which has monetary value—was stolen by *The Nation*. Though there would have been no copyright infringement involved in merely publishing the information, the use of a copyrighted expression of that information was not necessary to its dissemination and was purposely intended to prevent Harper & Row's licensee from being the first into print with it. Also, the fact that President Ford was a public figure did not mean that what he wrote had no protection under the copyright law.

Majority Opinion: Newsworthiness Does Not Justify Copyright Violation

Sandra Day O'Connor

*Sandra Day O'Connor was the first woman justice on the Su-
preme Court, where she served from 1981 until her retirement in
2006, and was considered a swing vote between its conservative
and liberal factions. In the following majority opinion she wrote
in* Harper & Row v. Nation, *she explains why the Court decided
that* The Nation's *unauthorized printing of excerpts from President Gerald Ford's memoirs did not come under the heading of
fair use. "Fair use" is a principle of copyright law that permits
the publishing of small portions of copyrighted material without
permission when certain conditions are met. Justice O'Connor
points out that in this case the conditions were not met, despite
the magazine's claim that the news value of the excerpt made
the use of it fair. If newsworthiness could override the normal
criteria for fair use, she says, there could never be any copyright
protection for the work of a public figure. Furthermore, the right
of an author to choose when and where to publish makes it less
fair to copy passages from an unpublished book than from a
published one.*

Sandra Day O'Connor, majority opinion, *Harper & Row, Publishers, Inc. v. Nation Enterprises*, U.S. Supreme Court, May 20, 1985. Reproduced by permission.

Article I, [Section] 8, of the Constitution provides: "The Congress shall have Power . . . to Promote the Progress of Science and useful Arts, by securing for limited Times to Authors and Inventors the exclusive Right to their respective Writings and Discoveries."

As we noted last Term:

> [This] limited grant is a means by which an important public purpose may be achieved. It is intended to motivate the creative activity of authors and inventors by the provision of a special reward, and to allow the public access to the products of their genius after the limited period of exclusive control has expired.

"The monopoly created by copyright thus rewards the individual author in order to benefit the public." This principle applies equally to works of fiction and nonfiction. The book at issue here, for example, was two years in the making, and began with a contract giving the author's copyright to the publishers in exchange for their services in producing and marketing the work. In preparing the book, Mr. [Gerald] Ford drafted essays and word portraits of public figures and participated in hundreds of taped interviews that were later distilled to chronicle his personal viewpoint. It is evident that the monopoly granted by copyright actively served its intended purpose of inducing the creation of new material of potential historical value. . . .

A Significant Right

The Nation has admitted to lifting verbatim quotes of the author's original language totaling between 300 and 400 words and constituting some 13% of *The Nation* article. In using generous verbatim excerpts of Mr. Ford's unpublished manuscript to lend authenticity to its account of the forthcoming memoirs, *The Nation* effectively arrogated to itself the right of first publication, an important marketable subsidiary right.

For the reasons set forth below, we find that this use of the copyrighted manuscript, even stripped to the verbatim quotes conceded by *The Nation* to be copyrightable expression, was not a fair use within the meaning of the Copyright Act....

Publication of an author's expression before he has authorized its dissemination seriously infringes the author's right to decide when and whether it will be made public, a factor not present in fair use of published works. Respondents contend, however, that Congress, in including first publication among the rights enumerated in [Section] 106 [of the Copyright Act], which are expressly subject to fair use under [Section] 107, intended that fair use would apply in *pari materia* [equally] to published and unpublished works. The Copyright Act does not support this proposition....

The right of first publication implicates a threshold decision by the author whether and in what form to release his work. First publication is inherently different from other [Section] 106 rights in that only one person can be the first publisher; as the contract with *Time* illustrates, the commercial value of the right lies primarily in exclusivity. Because the potential damage to the author from judicially enforced "sharing" of the first publication right with unauthorized users of his manuscript is substantial, the balance of equities in evaluating such a claim of fair use inevitably shifts....

The obvious benefit to author and public alike of assuring authors the leisure to develop their ideas free from fear of expropriation outweighs any short-term "news value" to be gained from premature publication of the author's expression. The author's control of first public distribution implicates not only his personal interest in creative control, but his property interest in exploitation of prepublication rights, which are valuable in themselves and serve as a valuable adjunct to publicity and marketing. Under ordinary circumstances, the author's right to control the first public appearance of his undisseminated expression will outweigh a claim of fair use.

News Value and Fair Use

Respondents, however, contend that First Amendment values require a different rule under the circumstances of this case. The thrust of the decision below is that "[t]he scope of [fair use] is undoubtedly wider when the information conveyed relates to matters of high public concern." Respondents advance the substantial public import of the subject matter of the Ford memoirs as grounds for excusing a use that would ordinarily not pass muster as a fair use—the piracy of verbatim quotations for the purpose of "scooping" the authorized first serialization. Respondents explain their copying of Mr. Ford's expression as essential to reporting the news story it claims the book itself represents. In respondents' view, not only the facts contained in Mr. Ford's memoirs, but "the precise manner in which [he] expressed himself [were] as newsworthy as what he had to say." Respondents argue that the public's interest in learning this news as fast as possible outweighs the right of the author to control its first publication. . . .

No author may copyright his ideas or the facts he narrates. As this Court long ago observed: "[T]he news element— the information respecting current events contained in the literary production—is not the creation of the writer, but is a report of matters that ordinarily are *publici juris*; it is the history of the day." But copyright assures those who write and publish factual narratives such as [Ford's book] *A Time to Heal* that they may at least enjoy the right to market the original expression contained therein as just compensation for their investment.

Respondents' theory, however, would expand fair use to effectively destroy any expectation of copyright protection in the work of a public figure. Absent such protection, there would be little incentive to create or profit in financing such memoirs, and the public would be denied an important source of significant historical information. The promise of copyright would be an empty one if it could be avoided merely by dubbing the infringement a fair use "news report" of the book.

Nor do respondents assert any actual necessity for circumventing the copyright scheme with respect to the types of works and users at issue here. Where an author and publisher have invested extensive resources in creating an original work and are poised to release it to the public, no legitimate aim is served by preempting the right of first publication. The fact that the words the author has chosen to clothe his narrative may of themselves be "newsworthy" is not an independent justification for unauthorized copying of the author's expression prior to publication. . . .

In our haste to disseminate news, it should not be forgotten that the Framers intended copyright itself to be the engine of free expression. By establishing a marketable right to the use of one's expression, copyright supplies the economic incentive to create and disseminate ideas. . . .

It is fundamentally at odds with the scheme of copyright to accord lesser rights in those works that are of greatest importance to the public. Such a notion ignores the major premise of copyright, and injures author and public alike. . . .

Moreover, freedom of thought and expression "includes both the right to speak freely and the right to refrain from speaking at all." We do not suggest this right not to speak would sanction abuse of the copyright owner's monopoly as an instrument to suppress facts. But in the words of New York's Chief Judge [Stanley] Fuld:

> The essential thrust of the First Amendment is to prohibit improper restraints on the voluntary public expression of ideas; it shields the man who wants to speak or publish when others wish him to be quiet. There is necessarily, and within suitably defined areas, a concomitant freedom not to speak publicly, one which serves the same ultimate end as freedom of speech in its affirmative aspect.

In view of the First Amendment protections already embodied in the Copyright Act's distinction between copyrightable expression and uncopyrightable facts and ideas, and the latitude for scholarship and comment traditionally afforded by fair use, we see no warrant for expanding the doctrine of fair use to create what amounts to a public figure exception to copyright. Whether verbatim copying from a public figure's manuscript in a given case is or is not fair must be judged according to the traditional equities of fair use. . . .

Determining Fair Use

The four factors identified by Congress as especially relevant in determining whether the use was fair are: (1) the purpose and character of the use; (2) the nature of the copyrighted work; (3) the substantiality of the portion used in relation to the copyrighted work as a whole; (4) the effect on the potential market for or value of the copyrighted work. We address each one separately.

Purpose of the Use. The Second Circuit correctly identified news reporting as the general purpose of *The Nation*'s use. . . . The fact that an article arguably is "news," and therefore a productive use, is simply one factor in a fair use analysis.

We agree with the Second Circuit that the trial court erred in fixing on whether the information contained in the memoirs was actually new to the public. . . .

The Nation has every right to seek to be the first to publish information. But *The Nation* went beyond simply reporting uncopyrightable information and actively sought to exploit the headline value of its infringement, making a "news event" out of its unauthorized first publication of a noted figure's copyrighted expression.

The fact that a publication was commercial, as opposed to nonprofit, is a separate factor that tends to weigh against a finding of fair use. "[E]very commercial use of copyrighted material is presumptively an unfair exploitation of the monopoly privilege that belongs to the owner of the copyright." In arguing that the purpose of news reporting is not purely commercial, *The Nation* misses the point entirely. The crux of the profit/nonprofit distinction is not whether the sole motive of the use is monetary gain, but whether the user stands to profit from exploitation of the copyrighted material without paying the customary price.

In evaluating character and purpose, we cannot ignore *The Nation*'s stated purpose of scooping the forthcoming hardcover and *Time* abstracts. *The Nation*'s use had not merely the incidental effect, but the intended purpose, of supplanting the copyright holder's commercially valuable right of first publication. . . . The trial court found that *The Nation* knowingly exploited a purloined manuscript. Unlike the typical claim of fair use, *The Nation* cannot offer up even the fiction of consent as justification. Like its competitor *newsweekly* [*Time*], it was free to bid for the right of abstracting excerpts from *A Time to Heal*. Fair use "distinguishes between 'a true scholar and a chiseler who infringes a work for personal profit.'"

Nature of the Copyrighted Work. Second, the Act directs attention to the nature of the copyrighted work. *A Time to Heal* may be characterized as an unpublished historical narrative or autobiography. The law generally recognizes a greater need to disseminate factual works than works of fiction or fantasy. . . .

Some of the briefer quotes from the memoirs are arguably necessary adequately to convey the facts; for example, Mr. Ford's characterization of the White House tapes as the "smoking gun" is perhaps so integral to the idea expressed as to be inseparable from it. But *The Nation* did not stop at isolated phrases, and instead excerpted subjective descriptions and portraits of public figures whose power lies in the author's individualized expression. Such use, focusing on the most expressive elements of the work, exceeds that necessary to disseminate the facts.

The fact that a work is unpublished is a critical element of its "nature." Our prior discussion establishes that the scope of fair use is narrower with respect to unpublished works. While even substantial quotations might qualify as fair use in a review of a published work or a news account of a speech that had been delivered to the public or disseminated to the press, the author's right to control the first public appearance of his expression weighs against such use of the work before its release. The right of first publication encompasses not only the choice whether to publish at all, but also the choices of when, where, and in what form first to publish a work.

In the case of Mr. Ford's manuscript, the copyright holders' interest in confidentiality is irrefutable; the copyright holders had entered into a contractual undertaking to "keep the manuscript confidential" and required that all those to whom the manuscript was shown also "sign an agreement to keep the manuscript confidential." While the copyright holders' contract with *Time* required *Time* to submit its proposed article seven days before publication, *The Nation*'s clandestine publication afforded no such opportunity for creative or quality control. It was hastily patched together, and contained "a number of inaccuracies" (testimony of [*Nation* editor] Victor Navasky). A use that so clearly infringes the copyright holder's interests in confidentiality and creative control is difficult to characterize as "fair."

Considerable Implications

Amount and Substantiality of the Portion Used. Next, the Act directs us to examine the amount and substantiality of the portion used in relation to the copyrighted work as a whole. In absolute terms, the words actually quoted were an insubstantial portion of *A Time to Heal.* The District Court, however, found that "[*T*]*he Nation* took what was essentially the heart of the book." We believe the Court of Appeals erred in overruling the District Judge's evaluation of the qualitative nature of the taking. A *Time* editor described the chapters on the pardon as "the most interesting and moving parts of the entire manuscript." The portions actually quoted were selected by Mr. Navasky as among the most powerful passages in those chapters. He testified that he used verbatim excerpts because simply reciting the information could not adequately convey the "absolute certainty with which [Ford] expressed himself" or show that "this comes from President Ford," or carry the "definitive quality" of the original. In short, he quoted these passages precisely because they qualitatively embodied Ford's distinctive expression.

As the statutory language indicates, a taking may not be excused merely because it is insubstantial with respect to the *infringing work*. As Judge Learned Hand cogently remarked, "no plagiarist can excuse the wrong by showing how much of his work he did not pirate." . . .

Effect on the Market. Finally, the Act focuses on "the effect of the use upon the potential market for or value of the copyrighted work." This last factor is undoubtedly the single most important element of fair use. The trial court found not merely a potential, but an actual, effect on the market. *Time*'s cancellation of its projected serialization and its refusal to pay the $12,500 were the direct effect of the infringement. The Court of Appeals rejected this factfinding as clearly erroneous, noting that the record did not establish a causal relation between *Time*'s nonperformance and respondents' unauthorized publication of Mr. Ford's *expression* as opposed to the facts taken from the memoirs. We disagree. Rarely will a case of copyright infringement present such clear-cut evidence of actual damage. Petitioners assured *Time* that there would be no other authorized publication of any portion of the unpublished manuscript prior to April 23, 1979. *Any* publication of material from chapters 1 and 3 would permit *Time* to renegotiate its final payment. *Time* cited *The Nation*'s article, which contained verbatim quotes from the unpublished manuscript, as a reason for its nonperformance. . . .

More important, to negate fair use, one need only show that, if the challenged use "should become widespread, it would adversely affect the *potential* market for the copyrighted work." This inquiry must take account not only of harm to the original, but also of harm to the market for derivative works. . . .

It is undisputed that the factual material in the balance of *The Nation's* article, besides the verbatim quotes at issue here, was drawn exclusively from the chapters on the pardon. The excerpts were employed as featured episodes in a story about the Nixon pardon—precisely the use petitioners had licensed to *Time*. The borrowing of these verbatim quotes from the unpublished manuscript lent *The Nation's* piece a special air of authenticity—as Navasky expressed it, the reader would know it was Ford speaking, and not *The Nation*. Thus it directly competed for a share of the market for prepublication excerpts. . . .

In sum, the traditional doctrine of fair use, as embodied in the Copyright Act, does not sanction the use made by *The Nation* of these copyrighted materials. Any copyright infringer may claim to benefit the public by increasing public access to the copyrighted work. But Congress has not designed, and we see no warrant for judicially imposing, a "compulsory license" permitting unfettered access to the unpublished copyrighted expression of public figures.

The Nation conceded that its verbatim copying of some 300 words of direct quotation from the Ford manuscript would constitute an infringement unless excused as a fair use. Because we find that *The Nation's* use of these verbatim excerpts from the unpublished manuscript was not a fair use, the judgment of the Court of Appeals is reversed, and the case is remanded for further proceedings consistent with this opinion.

Dissenting Opinion: Publication of the Disputed Material Was Fair Use

William J. Brennan

William J. Brennan was a justice of the Supreme Court from 1956 to 1990. He was a strong liberal who was influential in expanding the Court's view of individual rights. In his following dissenting opinion in Harper & Row v. Nation, *he argues that the excerpts from President Gerald Ford's memoirs published without permission by* The Nation *magazine consisted of ideas and facts, which cannot be copyrighted. Only the literary form in which an author has expressed ideas is protected by copyright, and in Justice Brennan's opinion, not enough of Ford's actual words appeared in the magazine to be considered infringement. Prohibiting immediate publication of newsworthy information will stifle the dissemination of ideas that copyright is meant to nurture, he says. He criticizes the majority of the Court for not distinguishing sufficiently between information and form, and declares that* The Nation *had every right to print the article it did. Although the premature publication caused the cancellation of the contract between Harper & Row and* Time *magazine,*

William J. Brennan, dissenting opinion, *Harper & Row, Publishers, Inc. v. Nation Enterprises*, U.S. Supreme Court, May 20, 1985.

Time's action was based not on the quotations printed but on the information in the article, which is not covered by copyright, and therefore Justice Brennan believes the publication was fair use.

The Court holds that *The Nation's* quotation of 300 words from the unpublished 200,000-word manuscript of President Gerald R. Ford infringed the copyright in that manuscript, even though the quotations related to a historical event of undoubted significance—the resignation and pardon of President Richard M. Nixon. Although the Court pursues the laudable goal of protecting "the economic incentive to create and disseminate ideas," this zealous defense of the copyright owner's prerogative will, I fear, stifle the broad dissemination of ideas and information copyright is intended to nurture. Protection of the copyright owner's economic interest is achieved in this case through an exceedingly narrow definition of the scope of fair use. The progress of arts and sciences and the robust public debate essential to an enlightened citizenry are ill-served by this constricted reading of the fair use doctrine. I therefore respectfully dissent. . . .

The challenge of copyright is to strike the "difficult balance between the interests of authors and inventors in the control and exploitation of their writings and discoveries, on the one hand, and society's competing interest in the free flow of ideas, information, and commerce, on the other hand."

The "originality" requirement now embodied in [Section] 102 of the Copyright Act is crucial to maintenance of the appropriate balance between these competing interests. Properly interpreted in the light of the legislative history, this section extends copyright protection to an author's literary form, but permits free use by others of the ideas and information the author communicates. This limitation of protection to literary form precludes any claim of copyright in facts, including historical narration.

It is not to be supposed that the framers of the Constitution, when they empowered Congress "to promote the progress of science and useful arts, by securing for limited times to authors and inventors the exclusive right to their respective writings and discoveries" intended to confer upon one who might happen to be the first to report a historic event the exclusive right for any period to spread the knowledge of it. [*International News Service v. Associated Press* (1918)]

The "promotion of science and the useful arts" requires this limit on the scope of an author's control. Were an author able to prevent subsequent authors from using concepts, ideas, or facts contained in his or her work, the creative process would wither and scholars would be forced into unproductive replication of the research of their predecessors. This limitation on copyright also ensures consonance with our most important First Amendment values. Our "profound national commitment to the principle that debate on public issues should be uninhibited, robust, and wide-open" [*New York Times Co. v. Sullivan* (1964)] leaves no room for a statutory monopoly over information and ideas. . . .

Ideas and Information Cannot Be Copyrighted

It follows that infringement of copyright must be based on a taking of literary form, as opposed to the ideas or information contained in a copyrighted work. Deciding whether an infringing appropriation of literary form has occurred is difficult for at least two reasons. First, the distinction between literary form and information or ideas is often elusive in practice. Second, infringement must be based on a substantial appropriation of literary form. This determination is equally challenging. Not surprisingly, the test for infringement has defied precise formulation. In general, though, the inquiry proceeds along two axes: *how closely* has the second author tracked the first author's particular language and structure of presentation; and *how much* of the first author's language and structure has the second author appropriated.

In the present case the infringement analysis must be applied to a historical biography in which the author has chronicled the events of his White House tenure and commented on those events from his unique perspective. Apart from the quotations, virtually all of the material in *The Nation*'s article indirectly recounted Mr. Ford's factual narrative of the Nixon resignation and pardon, his latter-day reflections on some events of his Presidency, and his perceptions of the personalities at the center of those events. No copyright can be claimed in this information *qua* [as] information. Infringement would thus have to be based on too close and substantial a tracking of Mr. Ford's expression of this information. . . .

The Language. Much of the information *The Nation* conveyed was not in the form of paraphrase at all, but took the form of synopsis of lengthy discussions in the Ford manuscript. In the course of this summary presentation, *The Nation* did use occasional sentences that closely resembled language in the original Ford manuscript. But these linguistic similarities are insufficient to constitute an infringement. . . . At most, *The Nation* paraphrased disparate isolated sentences from the original. A finding of infringement based on paraphrase generally requires far more close and substantial a tracking of the original language than occurred in this case.

The Structure of Presentation. The article does not mimic Mr. Ford's structure. The information *The Nation* presents is drawn from scattered sections of the Ford work, and does not appear in the sequence in which Mr. Ford presented it. Some of *The Nation*'s discussion of the pardon does roughly track the order in which the Ford manuscript presents information about the pardon. With respect to this similarity, however, Mr. Ford has done no more than present the facts chronologically and cannot claim infringement when a subsequent author similarly presents the facts of history in a chronological manner. Also, it is difficult to suggest that a 2,000-word article could bodily appropriate the structure of a 200,000-word book. Most of what Mr. Ford created, and most of the history he recounted, were simply not represented in *The Nation*'s article. . . .

Distinguishing Between Ideas and Form

With respect to a work of history, particularly the memoirs of a public official, the statutorily prescribed analysis cannot properly be conducted without constant attention to copyright's crucial distinction between protected literary form and unprotected information or ideas. The question must always be: was the subsequent author's use of literary form a fair use within the meaning of [Section] 107, in light of the purpose for the use, the nature of the copyrighted work, the amount of *literary form* used, and the effect of this use of literary form on the value of or market for the original?

Limiting the inquiry to the propriety of a subsequent author's use of the copyright owner's literary form is not easy in the case of a work of history. Protection against only substantial appropriation of literary form does not ensure historians a return commensurate with the full value of their labors. The literary form contained in works like [Ford's book] *A Time to Heal* reflects only a part of the labor that goes into the book. It is the labor of collecting, sifting, organizing, and reflecting that predominates in the creation of works of history such as this one. The value this labor produces lies primarily in the information and ideas revealed, and not in the particular collocation of words through which the information and ideas are expressed. Copyright thus does not protect that which is often of most value in a work of history, and courts must resist the tendency to reject the fair use defense on the basis of their feeling that an author of history has been deprived of the full value of his or her labor. A subsequent author's taking of information and ideas is in no sense piratical, because copyright law simply does not create any property interest in information and ideas. . . .

This distinction is at the essence of copyright. The copyright laws serve as the "engine of free expression" only when the statutory monopoly does not choke off multifarious indirect uses and consequent broad dissemination of information and ideas. To ensure the progress of arts and sciences and the integrity of First Amendment values, ideas and information must not be freighted with claims of proprietary right.

In my judgment, the Court's fair use analysis has fallen to the temptation to find copyright violation based on a minimal use of literary form in order to provide compensation for the appropriation of information from a work of history. The failure to distinguish between information and literary form permeates every aspect of the Court's fair use analysis, and leads the Court to the wrong result in this case. Application of the statutorily prescribed analysis with attention to the distinction between information and literary form leads to a straightforward finding of fair use within the meaning of [Section] 107.

News Reporting Can Be Fair Use

The Purpose of the Use. The Nation's purpose in quoting 300 words of the Ford manuscript was, as the Court acknowledges, news reporting. The Ford work contained information about important events of recent history. Two principals, Mr. Ford and General Alexander Haig, were, at the time of *The Nation's* publication in 1979, widely thought to be candidates for the Presidency. That *The Nation* objectively reported the information in the Ford manuscript without independent commentary in no way diminishes the conclusion that it was reporting news. A typical news story differs from an editorial precisely in that it presents newsworthy information in a straightforward and unelaborated manner. Nor does the source of the information render *The Nation's* article any less a news report. Often books and manuscripts, solicited and unsolicited, are the subject matter of news reports. Frequently, the manuscripts are unpublished at the time of the news report. . . .

The Court's reliance on the commercial nature of *The Nation*'s use as "a separate factor that tends to weigh against a finding of fair use" is inappropriate in the present context. Many uses [Section] 107 lists as paradigmatic examples of fair use, including criticism, comment, and *news reporting*, are generally conducted for profit in this country, a fact of which Congress was obviously aware when it enacted [Section] 107. To negate any argument favoring fair use based on news reporting or criticism because that reporting or criticism was published for profit is to render meaningless the congressional imprimatur placed on such uses.

Nor should *The Nation*'s intent to create a "news event" weigh against a finding of fair use. Such a rule, like the Court's automatic presumption against news reporting for profit, would undermine the congressional validation of the news reporting purpose. A news business earns its reputation, and therefore its readership, through consistent prompt publication of news—and often through "scooping" rivals. More importantly, the Court's failure to maintain the distinction between information and literary form colors the analysis of this point. Because Harper & Row had no legitimate copyright interest in the information and ideas in the Ford manuscript, *The Nation* had every right to seek to be the first to disclose these facts and ideas to the public. The record suggests only that *The Nation* sought to be the first to reveal the information in the Ford manuscript. *The Nation*'s stated purpose of scooping the competition should, under those circumstances, have no negative bearing on the claim of fair use. Indeed the Court's reliance on this factor would seem to amount to little more than distaste for the standard journalistic practice of seeking to be the first to publish news.

The Court's reliance on *The Nation*'s putative bad faith is equally unwarranted. No court has found that *The Nation* possessed the Ford manuscript illegally or in violation of any common law interest of Harper & Row; all common law causes of action have been abandoned or dismissed in this case. Even if the manuscript had been "purloined" by someone, nothing in this record imputes culpability to *The Nation*. On the basis of the record in this case, the most that can be said is that *The Nation* made use of the contents of the manuscript knowing the copyright owner would not sanction the use.

At several points the Court brands this conduct thievery. This judgment is unsupportable, and is perhaps influenced by the Court's unspoken tendency in this case to find infringement based on the taking of information and ideas.... Whether the quotation of 300 words was an infringement or a fair use within the meaning of Section 107 is a close question that has produced sharp division in both this Court and the Court of Appeals. If the Copyright Act were held not to prohibit the use, then the copyright owner would have had no basis in law for objecting. *The Nation*'s awareness of an objection that has a significant chance of being adjudged unfounded cannot amount to bad faith....

The Nature of the Copyrighted Work. In *Sony Corp. of America v. Universal City Studios, Inc.* [in which the Supreme Court ruled VCR use for the purposes of time-shifting to be fair use], we stated that "not ... all copyrights are fungible" and that "[c]opying a news broadcast may have a stronger claim to fair use than copying a motion picture." These statements reflect the principle, suggested in [Section] 107(2) of the Act, that the scope of fair use is generally broader when the source of borrowed expression is a factual or historical work.

The Court acknowledges that "[t]he law generally recognizes a greater need to disseminate factual works than works of fiction or fantasy," and that "[s]ome of the briefer quotations from the memoir are arguably necessary to convey the facts." But the Court discounts the force of this consideration, primarily on the ground that "[t]he fact that a work is unpublished is a crucial element of its 'nature.'" At this point, the Court introduces into analysis of this case a categorical presumption against prepublication fair use. This categorical presumption is unwarranted on its own terms and unfaithful to congressional intent. . . .

The Court Relies on Speculation

To the extent the Court purports to evaluate the facts of this case, its analysis relies on sheer speculation. The quotation of 300 words from the manuscript infringed no privacy interest of Mr. Ford. This author intended the words in the manuscript to be a public statement about his Presidency. Lacking, therefore, is the "deliberate choice on the part of the copyright owner" to keep expression confidential, a consideration that the Senate Report—in the passage on which the Court places great reliance—recognized as the impetus behind narrowing fair use for unpublished works. What the Court depicts as the copyright owner's "confidentiality" interest is not a privacy interest at all. Rather, it is no more than an economic interest in capturing the full value of initial release of information to the public, and is properly analyzed as such. Lacking too is any suggestion that *The Nation*'s use interfered with the copyright owner's interest in editorial control of the manuscript. *The Nation* made use of the Ford quotes on the eve of official publication. . . .

The Amount and Substantiality of the Portion Used. More difficult questions arise with respect to judgments about the importance to this case of the amount and substantiality of the quotations used. *The Nation* quoted only approximately 300 words from a manuscript of more than 200,000 words, and the quotes are drawn from isolated passages in disparate sections of the work. The judgment that this taking was quantitatively "infinitesimal" does not dispose of the inquiry, however. An evaluation of substantiality in qualitative terms is also required. Much of the quoted material was Mr. Ford's matter-of-fact representation of the words of others in conversations with him; such quotations are "arguably necessary adequately to convey the facts" and are not rich in expressive content. Beyond these quotations, a portion of the quoted material was drawn from the most poignant expression in the Ford manuscript; in particular *The Nation* made use of six examples of Mr. Ford's expression of his reflections on events or perceptions about President Nixon. The fair use inquiry turns on the propriety of the use of these quotations with admittedly strong expressive content.

The Court holds that, "in view of the expressive value of the excerpts and their key role in the infringing work," this third statutory factor disfavors a finding of fair use. To support this conclusion, the Court purports to rely on the District Court factual findings that *The Nation* had taken "the heart of the book." This reliance is misplaced, and would appear to be another result of the Court's failure to distinguish between information and literary form. When the District Court made this finding, it was evaluating not the quoted words at issue here, but the "totality" of the information and reflective commentary in the Ford work. The vast majority of what the District Court considered the heart of the Ford work, therefore, consisted of ideas and information *The Nation* was free to use. . . .

At least with respect to the six particular quotes of Mr. Ford's observations and reflections about President Nixon, I agree with the Court's conclusion that *The Nation* appropriated some literary form of substantial quality. I do not agree, however, that the substantiality of the expression taken was clearly excessive or inappropriate to *The Nation*'s news reporting purpose.

Had these quotations been used in the context of a critical book review of the Ford work, there is little question that such a use would be fair use within the meaning of [Section] 107 of the Act. The amount and substantiality of the use—both quantitative and qualitative terms—would have certainly been appropriate to the purpose of such a use. It is difficult to see how the use of these quoted words in a news report is less appropriate. . . .

The Effect on the Market. The Court correctly notes that the effect on the market "is undoubtedly the single most important element of fair use." And the Court properly focuses on whether *The Nation's* use adversely affected Harper & Row's serialization potential and not merely the market for sales of the Ford work itself. Unfortunately, the Court's failure to distinguish between the use of information and the appropriation of literary form badly skews its analysis of this factor. . . .

The Nation's publication indisputably precipitated *Time's* eventual cancellation. But that does not mean that *The Nation's* use of the 300 quoted words caused this injury to Harper & Row. Wholly apart from these quoted words, *The Nation* published significant information and ideas from the Ford manuscript. If it was this publication of information, and not the publication of the few quotations, that caused *Time* to abrogate its serialization agreement, then whatever the negative effect on the serialization market, that effect was the product of wholly legitimate activity. . . .

Because *The Nation* was the first to convey the information in this case, it did perhaps take from Harper & Row some of the value that publisher sought to garner for itself through the contractual arrangement with Ford and the license to *Time*. Harper & Row had every right to seek to monopolize revenue from that potential market through contractual arrangements, but it has no right to set up copyright as a shield from competition in that market, because copyright does not protect information. *The Nation* had every right to seek to be the first to publish that information.

Balancing the Interests. Once the distinction between information and literary form is made clear, the statutorily prescribed process of weighing the four statutory fair use factors discussed above leads naturally to a conclusion that *The Nation*'s limited use of literary form was not an infringement. . . .

The Court imposes liability upon *The Nation* for no other reason than that *The Nation* succeeded in being the first to provide certain information to the public.

The Court Protected Commercial Interests at the Expense of Free Dissemination of Facts

Slade Metcalf

Slade Metcalf is an attorney who specializes in representing publishers, radio and TV stations, movie studios, and authors. In the following viewpoint he describes the dispute between the publisher Harper & Row and The Nation *magazine, which resulted in a Supreme Court ruling that it is not fair use for news media to print excerpts from unpublished books without permission from the copyright holder. Former president Gerald Ford had arranged for Harper & Row to publish his memoirs and for an excerpt to appear in* Time *magazine, but* The Nation *got hold of the manuscript and printed some of it before* Time *had a chance to do so. Therefore,* Time *was not obliged to pay the amount to Harper & Row that had been agreed upon, and because the book publisher and author lost this money, the Court ruled that* The Nation's *action could not be considered fair use. Metcalf explains the criteria that determine whether a use is considered fair under the copyright law. In his opinion, they were interpreted too strictly. Only a small section of the manuscript was printed ahead of time, and its content was newsworthy, so he feels the Court should have given more consideration to* The Nation's *effort to get the information to the public at the earliest possible date.*

Magazine publishers are asking their lawyers, "How are we affected by the Supreme Court's decision in *The Nation* case?" "Are we now prohibited from quoting from published books?" "Has investigative journalism suffered a mortal blow?"

Although the second and third questions can be answered with a simple "no," the first question requires an extended explanation—which in turn demands a working familiarity with the underlying facts of *The Nation* case.

In February 1977, Harper & Row and *Reader's Digest* entered into a publishing agreement with former President Gerald R. Ford for his memoirs. (Harper & Row was to be the book publisher and *Reader's Digest* apparently acquired second serial rights.) Over the next two years, Mr. Ford, with the assistance of Trevor Ambrister, a senior editor at *Reader's Digest*, wrote a 200,000-word manuscript that totaled 655 pages. Harper & Row and *Reader's Digest* retained the exclusive licensing rights to the manuscript, which was to be called *A Time To Heal*. Harper & Row was protective of these rights and, by agreement, restricted Mr. Ford from disclosing the contents of the book prior to the publication date.

In March 1979, the publishers sold first serial rights in the book to *Time* for $25,000—$12,500 in advance and the balance at publication. *Time* could excerpt up to 7,500 words from the book, but reserved the right to renegotiate the price prior to the second payment if the material from the manuscript appeared in print prior to *Time's* on-sale date. The *Time* excerpt was to be on sale (April 16) about one week before the books would be shipped to bookstores.

About two to three weeks prior to *Time*'s scheduled on-sale date, Victor Navasky, editor of *The Nation*, received an unsolicited copy of the unpublished manuscript. In the well-established tradition of competitive journalism, Navasky composed an article based exclusively on the contents of *A Time To Heal*, liberally quoting from the manuscript. *The Nation* published the 2,250-word article on April 3, 1979, which was 13 days prior to *Time*'s publication date.

Time asked that Harper & Row permit it to print the excerpt in its issue on stands on April 9 rather than April 16, but Harper & Row refused. *Time* then invoked its rights under its agreement with Harper & Row, decided not to publish the excerpt, and declined to pay the remaining $12,500.

Suing *The Nation*

Harper & Row and *Reader's Digest* then sued *The Nation* for copyright infringement and other state law violations. The trial judge, hearing the case without a jury, ruled in favor of the copyright owners and awarded them $12,500 in damages as a result of *The Nation*'s infringement of the publishers' copyright. *The Nation* appealed to the United States Court of Appeals, which, in a 2-1 decision, reversed the trial court and dismissed the complaint. The Supreme Court agreed to hear the case and on May 20, 1985, in a 6-3 ruling, reversed the Court of Appeals by finding that *The Nation* had indeed infringed the publishers' copyright.

The majority of the Supreme Court, speaking through Justice [Sandra Day] O'Connor, was aghast at the conduct of Navasky and *The Nation* in obtaining the manuscript and publishing the article. The majority ridiculed Navasky's conduct by implying that a "scoop" was a seamy aspect of the journalism profession; by noting that Navasky claimed in his deposition that the article was "a real hot news story" when, in fact, most of the information had been previously published; and by stating that *The Nation* "had knowingly exploited a purloined manuscript."

In reacting to the pejorative reference to the practice of "scooping," the dissenting opinion, written by Justice [William J.] Brennan, commented: "A news business earns its reputation, and therefore its readership, through consistent prompt publication of news—and often through 'scooping' rivals. . . . Indeed the Court's reliance on this factor would seem to amount to little more than distaste for the standard journalistic practice of seeking to be the first to publish news."

Contrary to the majority's sense of indignation with *The Nation*'s appropriation of the publisher's property, the dissent and the intermediate appellate court properly pointed out that *The Nation* did not possess the manuscript illegally nor did it participate in the "theft" of the manuscript. Navasky neither solicited nor paid for the delivery of the manuscript. He was not aware at the time he received the manuscript that *Time* had acquired first rights in it, although he subsequently learned of it prior to publication. He conceded that he was not authorized to see or have possession of the manuscript. That, by itself, however, was not a violation of any law.

Applying "Fair Use"

With the Court's bias against this type of journalistic practice as a backdrop, the majority analyzed the Copyright Act and focused on the provision dealing with "fair use." The Copyright Act is premised on the concept that facts and information are not protectable or copyrightable—only the expression of those facts can be copyrighted. At the same time, republication of other persons' statements or of government documents is not copyrightable.

The Nation admitted that it used verbatim quotes from the book totaling 300 to 400 words, which constituted some 13 percent of *The Nation*'s article. It amounted to approximately less than two-tenths of 1 percent of the total words in *A Time To Heal*. Even this minimal use of copyrighted material is a violation of the Copyright Act unless the use can be deemed "fair" as delineated by the Act.

"Fair use" has historically been invoked as a defense to a copyright suit on the theory that the author or creator of the work would have given his or her consent to the reasonable and responsible use had he or she been asked. Fair use was often recognized when the quoted portions of the work were in the context of noncommercial, editorial, educational or charitable purposes. Frequently, nonlawyers would focus on the number of words that were copied from the article or book before deciding to ask the copyright owner for permission to print the material. A thoroughly discredited but oft-employed rule of thumb was that an amount under 50 words could be taken without requesting permission.

In enacting the new Copyright Act in 1976, Congress imposed some structure on the courts' and the public's determination of whether a use was "fair." Section 107 of the Act now provides four factors to be considered in deciding whether the unauthorized use was fair: 1) the purpose and character of the use; 2) the nature of the copyrighted work; 3) the substantiality of the portion used in relation to the copyrighted work as a whole; and 4) the effect on the potential market for or value of the copyrighted work.

The majority of the Court emphasized that unauthorized publication of an unpublished manuscript was a critical factor in negating the defense of fair use. "Under ordinary circumstances, the author's right to control the first public appearance of his undisseminated expression will outweigh a claim of fair use."

Safeguarding Economic Value

The majority of the Court was clearly fixated on the publishers' and Gerald Ford's right to safeguard the economic value in their copyrighted manuscript at the expense of the First Amendment values inherent in *The Nation*'s effort to disseminate information of substantial public importance at the earliest possible date. The Court's implied response that the public needed to wait only a few weeks for the same information to appear in the pages of *Time* or the book itself is an empty excuse—particularly when the free disclosure of newsworthy facts is at issue rather than the limited, verbatim republication of the expression of those facts. As the dissenting justices argued, "Harper & Row had every right to seek to monopolize revenue from that potential market through contractual arrangements, but it has no right to set up copyright [as] a shield from competition in the market because copyright does not protect information. *The Nation* had every right to seek to be the first to publish that information."

The majority of the justices considered the four factors of Section 107. They concluded that, in view of the unpublished nature of the manuscript, *The Nation*'s intended purpose of "scooping" the competition, the "clandestine publication" by the magazine, the 300 words taken not being an infinitesimal amount of the book, and the materially adverse effect of the article upon the market for first serial rights, the use by *The Nation* was not fair.

What are the lessons for magazine people from *Harper & Row, Publishers, Inc. vs. Nation Enterprises*? The protection to first serial rights has been effectively enhanced. The fact that the author of a copyrighted book or article is a high-level public official does not permit a publisher to use quoted material at will. On the other hand, a book reviewer still has substantial leeway in quoting from the published book or paraphrasing significant portions of the book to provide his or her literary analysis. Reuse of facts and information from copyrighted works is still protected provided the magazine writer does not employ the precise expression from the book or article in conveying those facts.

In light of these results, the legal and journalistic impact of *The Nation* case may be quite limited, since the need to quote exactly and extensively from unpublished yet copyrighted works is infrequent. The more troubling aspect of *The Nation* opinion is the Supreme Court's predilection toward protecting commercial interests at the expense of curtailing the free and open dissemination of facts and ideas.

Harper & Row was understandably incensed that *The Nation* had disrupted its exclusive arrangement with *Time*. However, Harper & Row surely anticipated that the breach of confidentiality could arise, since it permitted in its agreement that *Time* could back out of the deal. A lawsuit under the rubric of copyright was really not the answer to protect its interests. Three hundred words out of a 600-page book should hardly amount to unfair use.

> "In the hands of an editor with magazines to sell, the First Amendment becomes, in the name of freedom, an instrument of coercion."

The Right to Free Speech Includes a Right to Choose Where to Speak

George F. Will

George Will is a well known columnist and a political commentator on ABC television. In the following viewpoint, he comments sarcastically on the action of The Nation *magazine in printing an excerpt from Gerald Ford's unpublished memoirs without permission and claiming, when sued by the holder of the copyright, that under the First Amendment the information should not be withheld for private profit. In Will's opinion* The Nation *published the material for its own profit—that is, to sell magazines. The Supreme Court ruling on* Harper & Row v. Nation, *he notes, pointed out that the First Amendment not only protects a person's freedom to express ideas, but also protects an author's freedom to decide when and where to express them, and publishing them without permission is a denial of this freedom. Will agrees with the decision because it recognized authors' rights and restricted the alleged rights of news organizations to publish material as fast as they can get it. He suggests that advocates of property rights should be grateful to* The Nation *for having caused the Court to rule on the issue.*

*T*he *Nation* magazine is of stern left-wing views, and is brimful of disdain for the profit motives of capitalist civilization. Its editors no doubt feel deep pain because they must (this sad world enforces moral compromise) put a price on their product rather than give it away at newsstands, to each according to need.

But being an uncompromising critic of bourgeois values, *The Nation* never bends its knee to the totem of private property. So it was with the pleasure that comes when ideological and commercial considerations converge, that *The Nation* expropriated Gerald Ford's memoirs, for profit and, of course, for terribly high principle. The result was litigation and now a Supreme Court ruling more entertaining than historic, but entertaining because it illustrates the American left's knack for mashing its thumb with its own hammer.

In 1979 *Time* magazine was poised to publish a 7,500-word extract from Ford's forthcoming memoirs. *Time* had already paid $12,500 and was to pay another $12,500 upon publication. But shortly before *Time*'s publication date, an undisclosed source provided *The Nation* with a manuscript of the memoirs.

The Nation rushed into print a 2,250 word article based on, and quoting 300 words from, the portion of the memoirs *Time* had especially wanted, dealing with Ford's pardon of Nixon. Exclusivity having been lost, *Time* cancelled publication plans and the second payment. Harper & Row, Ford's publisher and holder of the copyright, sued *The Nation* for copyright infringement.

A district court held for Harper & Row, but an appeals court reversed. It held that authors can copyright their "expression" but not facts and ideas, least of all "politically significant" facts and ideas such as those *The Nation* reported as news. The appeals court said copyright law should not "impede the harvest of knowledge" or "kill the activities of the press."

The Purpose of Copyright Laws

But the Supreme Court, divided 6-3, has reversed the appeals court's reversal, holding that to treat as acceptable what *The Nation* did would defeat the intent of copyright laws. That intent is to promote knowledge by guaranteeing a fair return to those who augment knowledge. The interest of book publishers and authors have here prevailed over the interests of those who publish journalism.

The Nation's editor, cloaking his professional and commercial interests in the cloth of public-spiritedness, and dressing up his defeat as a blow to the public weal, says the Court's decision allows public officials "to withhold public information, the news, for private profit," and this "undermines the public's right to know."

Note how in the hands of an editor with magazines to sell, the First Amendment becomes, in the name of freedom, an instrument of coercion. According to *The Nation's* editor, the First Amendment licenses him to determine that a person—at least a public person—must speak, and when.

Writing for the Court's majority, Justice Sandra Day O'Connor notes that the fundamental purpose of the First Amendment is to prevent improper restrictions on voluntary public expression of ideas. It protects the individual's right to speak when others want him to be quiet. But there is a concomitant freedom to refrain from expressing oneself until one wants to do so. *The Nation* denied that freedom to Ford, at a financial cost to him.

Justice William Brennan, joined by Justices Byron White and Thurgood Marshall, dissented, arguing that the Court's construction of copyright law will "stifle the broad dissemination of ideas and information that copyright is intended to nurture." *The Nation's* lawyer, not to be outdone in wringing apocalyptic portent from this little case, says the ruling "is basically a denial to the public of the most important information about their government unless and until it is sold to them by a former public official."

Actually, the decision was of narrow scope, turning, in part, on *The Nation*'s use of verbatim quotations, which were not essential to *The Nation*'s reporting of facts. But the decision constitutes a modest enhancement of a property right and a corresponding modest restriction on the right of news organizations to publish newsworthy material as quickly as they get it. Friends of property rights should send thank you notes to *The Nation*.

For nearly two decades, life has been like that for the American left. The left's principal accomplishment is the ascendancy, political and intellectual, of the right, which grew in reaction to the excesses of the left.

"No two judges ever seem to agree on the application of fair use, and fair use cases are always bumping up against the First Amendment."

The Fair Use Exemption to Copyright Depends on Factors Specific to Each Case

Jack Shafer

Jack Shafer is editor at large for Slate, *an online magazine. In the following article he contends that although both Hillary Clinton and J.K. Rowling have considered suing the press for printing unauthorized excerpts from their newest books prior to publication, their cases do not follow the circumstances of* Harper & Row v. Nation. *The latter is frequently viewed as a precedent in such cases, but in Shafer's opinion it was less a landmark case than a subjective decision by the justices that is not applicable to many other "fair use" cases. Furthermore, Clinton's and Rowling's cases are different from* Nation *in many ways. The newspaper quotations from Clinton's book did not result in* Time *backing out of its agreement to buy the rights to print an excerpt, as it had in* Nation. *The newspaper that revealed part of* Harry Potter and the Order of the Phoenix *had not obtained an unauthorized manuscript; it simply bought a copy of the book from a retailer who mistakenly made it available prior to the official publication date. And neither author can claim that premature printing of passages interfered with book sales, since both of their*

Jack Shafer, "Embargo Nazis: Hillary Clinton's and J.K. Rowling's Publishers Are All Wet About Copyright," *Slate*, June 26, 2003. Reprinted with permission.

books have sold exceptionally well. They and their publishers should be grateful, Shafer says, for the advance publicity the premature publication provided.

Hillary Rodham Clinton's and J.K. Rowling's publishers howled at the press [in June 2003] for jumping the publication "embargoes" they'd placed on the release of *Living History* and *Harry Potter and Order of the Phoenix*. Clinton's publisher, Simon & Schuster, was contemplating a lawsuit against the Associated Press [AP] for publishing findings and quotations from her book six days before its official publication date. J.K. Rowling and her publisher went beyond threats, serving the *New York Daily News* with a $100 million copyright infringement lawsuit. The *Daily News* published plot details from Rowling's latest and reproduced two pages from it verbatim three days before the book's official June 21 release. Rowling's attorneys angrily jawboned *USA Today* and the Associated Press for publishing reviews of *Phoenix* prior to the official pub date, but filed no suits. Yet.

Clinton and Rowling may honestly believe the press violated their copyrights by quoting from and discussing the contents of their books prior to the official pub date. But neither author has much of a legal case, and I'm sure their lawyers would confess over drinks that the noise and litigation is mostly theater.

At the core of Clinton's and Rowling's kvetching [complaining] is the legal concept of "right of first publication," which under U.S. copyright law belongs to the copyright holders. In news roundups about both the Clinton and Rowling episodes, journalists knowingly pointed to the "landmark" copyright infringement case of *Harper & Row v. Nation Enterprises*, decided by the Supreme Court in 1985, to illustrate the writers' complaints. But the problem with citing *Harper & Row v. Nation* as legal precedent is that it's less a landmark decision than a somewhat capricious one-off opinion by the high court.

In 1979, *The Nation* jumped an embargo on President Gerald R. Ford's memoir, *A Time To Heal*. Having obtained a purloined copy of the manuscript, the magazine printed a 2,250-word article decanting the book's most newsworthy elements just before *Time* planned to publish an excerpt, for which it had promised to pay $12,500 in advance and $12,500 upon publication. Because it had been scooped, *Time* canceled its excerpt after the *Nation* piece appeared, and Ford's publisher, Harper & Row, sued *The Nation* for copyright infringement, among other things. What strengthened Harper & Row's case was that it could point to lost business and demonstrable financial damages, which isn't always true in copyright infringement cases. (The excerpt contract permitted *Time* to renege on the final $12,500 installment if material from the book appeared first elsewhere.)

A Fuzzy Area of Law

In its legal defense, *The Nation* invoked the "fair use" exemption to copyright laws, a murky and fuzzy area of the law. No two judges ever seem to agree on the application of fair use, and fair use cases are always bumping up against the First Amendment.

Essentially, fair use allows the reproduction of a *limited* amount of a copyrighted work—book symphony, magazine article, speech, map, photograph, etc.—commentary, criticism, news reporting, parody, noncommercial use in a classroom, etc., as long as it doesn't usurp the so-called value of the work or pre-empt the copyright-holders' right of first publication.

But how much is a limited amount? What is a parody or commentary? What's commercial use? What's educational? What's news reporting? How do you judge whether the value of a work has been usurped? What constitutes a violation of the right of first publication? This subjective and maddeningly inconsistent terrain makes you glad you never studied law. The only thing that's clear is that "one size fits all" does not apply to infringement cases, which means the only place to settle fair use disputes once and for all is in court, where judges repeatedly decide them on a case-by-case basis.

Although journalists bring up *Harper & Row v. Nation* as the important precedent every time a newspaper or magazine publishes something from a work yet to be officially published, the circumstance of the case and the waffling application of fair use in general indicate how completely subjective such cases are. The lower courts disagreed about *Harry & Row v. Nation* before the Supreme Court finally decided 6-3 in favor of Harper & Row, and even the Supreme Court ruling was anything but a slam dunk. In his dissenting opinion, Justice William Brennan argued:

> this zealous defense of the copyright owner's prerogative will, I fear, stifle the broad dissemination of ideas and information copyright is intended to nurture. Protection of the copyright owner's economic interest is achieved in this case through an exceedingly narrow definition of the scope of fair use. The progress of arts and sciences and the robust public debate essential to an enlightened citizenry are ill served by this constricted reading of the fair use doctrine.

Had the circumstance of the case been only slightly different, or the cast of the court subtly changed, the case could have gone to *The Nation* without anyone blinking.

As one intellectual property attorney told me, most fair use cases boil down to whether the court likes or dislikes the defendants. Reading Justice Sandra Day O'Connor's decision, you can smell her fury at *The Nation* lefties.

Harper & Row won its case against *The Nation* for a handful of specific reasons: 1) The magazine admitted it got its information from a purloined copy of the Ford manuscript, making them look like scoundrels if not thieves; 2) its story was explicitly timed to pre-empt the news value of the announced *Time* excerpt; 3) the article all but gloated that it was negating the copyright-holders' commercially valuable "right of first publication"; 4) *The Nation* could have reported uncopyrightable material, the court noted, but chose to quote 300-plus copyrighted words directly from the unpublished book and in doing so "actively sought to exploit the headline value of its infringement, making a 'news event'" out of its piece; and 5) because *Time* had called off its *A Time To Heal* serial, Harper & Row could point to real, rather than hypothetical, financial damages. This is a big deal, because in many infringement cases it's hard to put a dollar figure on damages.

Clinton and Rowling Cases Differ

If suits by Clinton and Rowling go to court, *Harper & Row v. Nation* would guide the judges' thinking only to the degree that the case resembles *Harper & Row v. Nation*. But aside from the publishers and authors wanting the media to regard embargo dates as legally enforceable under the rights-of-first-publication maxim, there isn't much overlap.

Take Clinton's book. The AP story limited direct quotation from the Clinton book to only 180 words. Unlike *The Nation*, which gloated over its scoop, the AP didn't tweak *Time*, once again the purchaser of serial rights for the book, and *Time* published its excerpt, so Simon & Schuster can't point to precise financial damage. Neither did the AP story suck all the news value out of Clinton's book, as *The Nation*'s story pretty much did.

If Rowling and her publishers, Scholastic, want to accuse the *Daily News* of violating their right of first publication, they're going to have a tougher time of it than Harper & Row did. The *Daily News* acquired its copy of the book at a Brooklyn health-food store that put it on sale, by mistake, before the June 21 publisher's embargo. (A number of retailers around the country made the same mistake.) Scholastic might have a case against the health-food store or the distributors, if they signed contracts pledging not to sell the book before June 21. But the buyer of *Harry Potter and the of the Phoenix* doesn't bear the legal consequences when the retailer screws up. Books traditionally dribble into stores weeks before or after their official publication dates. Can we really consider a book "unpublished" when copies are available for purchase in stores? (The AP didn't indicate how it obtained a copy of the Clinton book, leaving the publishers to guess.)

Rowling would be smarter to argue that the *Daily News* exceeded fair use doctrine in reproducing two pages, or about 940-words, straight out of the 870-page book. The law specifies no number of words that one can quote from a book in a review, but most publications limit themselves to 250 or 300. The 940 words the *Daily News* publish exceeds the standard rule of thumb for quotations, but it's only about 0.23 percent of the complete book. Would a court find this a violation of fair use? Especially if the two pages weren't all that integral to the plot? I doubt it. And would Rowling's attorneys—or Clinton's, for that matter—be prepared to argue that the AP and *Daily News* damaged sales with their stories? No way: *Harry Potter and the Order of the Phoenix* is breaking records and sales of [Clinton's] *Living History* are approaching the half-million mark.

The Desire to Control Publicity

The legal saber rattling has more to do with the publishers' desire to control what people write about forthcoming books before they are "officially" published so that publishers can reap the gains of their publicity campaigns, as David D. Kirkpatrick noted over the weekend in the *New York Times*. In other words, they want to release books the way Hollywood releases movies.

The courts have long placed more fair use restrictions on unpublished work than on published work. But the right of first publication is never absolute, as the majority in *Harper & Row v. Nation* conceded. In his dissent, Justice Brennan suggested that the court ask these questions before deciding a right of first-publication fair-use case. What kind of copyrighted work is it? What was the timing of the prepublication? What medium did the prepublication appear in? Did the prepublication usurp all value from a copyright owner's first right of publication?

"[C]ertain uses might be tolerable for some purposes but not for others," Brennan wrote.

Publishers who tempt their audiences with hype-filled publicity campaigns can't complain if journalists and audiences act prematurely on those aroused appetites. They should be grateful for the advance publicity now and again, especially when the press doesn't pinch more of their content than they would in a review published after the official pub date. Finally, if releasing a book at a precise date and time is so financially important to the embargo Nazis, let them shoulder the security costs. Don't punish the press just because publishers' plans have gone askew.

On the other hand, if you copy so much as [a] word from this column without permission, you'll be hearing from the amateur lawyer who [writes it.]

CHAPTER 3

The Copyright Term Extension Act of 1998 Is Not Unconstitutional

Case Overview

Eldred v. Ashcroft (2003)

In 1998 Congress passed the Copyright Term Extension Act (CTEA), also known as the Sonny Bono Copyright Term Extension Act, which extended the duration of copyright. Previously, copyrights had lasted fifty years after the creator's death, or in the case of copyrights held by companies, seventy-five years after a work's publication. The CTEA added twenty years to these terms, and the new terms applied not only to new copyrights but to those already in existence.

This struck many people as an unnecessary law. Why would authors care about copyright protection lasting seventy years after their death instead of fifty? Most authors do not expect their books to remain popular long enough for that to matter to their heirs. Moreover, it was not the authors who sought the extension—although some songwriters did, such as Sonny Bono and the heirs of George Gershwin. It was pushed through by corporate copyright owners—notably the Walt Disney Company, which lobbied extensively for the extension because its copyright on Mickey Mouse was about to expire. For this reason, critics often refer to it as the Mickey Mouse Protection Act.

The official purpose of the CTEA was to make U.S. copyright terms the same as those in the European Union and thereby maintain America's position in international trade. It was also argued that copyright was intended to protect at least one generation of an author's heirs, and that because people live longer now than in the past, fifty years is not long enough to last that generation's lifetime.

The CTEA was widely opposed by scholarly groups, libraries, and other organizations because they had been expecting works from the 1920s and 1930s to fall into the public domain soon, allowing them to be reproduced without permission. Such organizations, especially those creating large databases, usually cannot afford to pay fees for old works—and in any case, permissions are hard to obtain because the authors or their heirs often cannot be located.

One of the people who objected to the law was Eric Eldred, who maintained a Web site on which he made great literature from the past available free to the public and who had planned to add some books for which the copyright had been scheduled to expire. He agreed to be the lead plaintiff in a lawsuit claiming that the CTEA was unconstitutional. The suit did not contest the longer term for new copyrights, but argued that because the Constitution authorizes the creation of a copyright for "limited time" only, the limit for existing copyrights cannot exceed the one in effect at the time they were created. It also contended that copyright regulates free speech and thus must be subjected to the strict judicial scrutiny required in cases involving the First Amendment.

The district court held that the CTEA does not violate the "limited time" restriction of the Constitution's copyright clause because the CTEA's terms are still limited, not perpetual. It also held that there are no First Amendment rights to use the copyrighted works of others. The appellate court affirmed this decision, ruling that copyright does not impermissibly restrict free speech because it does not cover ideas or facts, but only an author's expression of them.

When the Supreme Court reviewed the case, it upheld the earlier rulings by a vote of seven to two. Although much of the discussion concerned the issue of whether or not extending copyright was wise, that issue, the Court believed, was for Congress to decide. The Court had authority only to determine whether Congress had the right to pass the law, and the majority believed that the Constitution did give it that right.

> "In addition to spurring the creation
> and publication of new expression,
> copyright law contains built-in First
> Amendment accommodations."

Majority Opinion: Congress Has the Authority to Set the Copyright Term

Ruth Bader Ginsburg

Ruth Bader Ginsburg has been a justice of the Supreme Court since 1993 and is one of its most liberal members. The following is the opinion she wrote in Eldred v. Ashcroft, *a case in which the petitioners argued that the Copyright Term Extension Act (CTEA) was unconstitutional. In it she explains why the majority of the Court did not agree with this argument. Congress had the authority, she says, to set limited terms for copyright protection, and contrary to the assertion of the petitioners, a term is still limited if Congress extends it for existing copyright holders, as well as setting a longer term for new copyrights. Furthermore, the Copyright Clause of the Constitution was adopted at about the same time as the First Amendment, which shows that the Framers believed it was compatible with the principle of free speech. The petitioners maintain that extending the term of copyrights is bad policy, but that is not for the Court to decide, says Ginsburg. The power to do that is given to Congress by the Constitution.*

Ruth Bader Ginsburg, majority opinion, *Eldred v. Ashcroft*, U.S. Supreme Court, January 15, 2003.

W e address first the determination of the courts below that Congress has authority under the Copyright Clause to extend the terms of existing copyrights. Text, history, and precedent, we conclude, confirm that the Copyright Clause empowers Congress to prescribe "limited times" for copyright protection and to secure the same level and duration of protection for all copyright holders, present and future.

The CTEA's baseline term of life plus 70 years, petitioners concede, qualifies as a "limited Tim[e]" as applied to future copyrights. Petitioners contend, however, that existing copyrights extended to endure for that same term are not "limited." Petitioners' argument essentially reads into the text of the Copyright Clause the command that a time prescription, once set, becomes forever "fixed" or "inalterable." The word "limited," however, does not convey a meaning so constricted. . . . A time span appropriately "limited" as applied to future copyrights does not automatically cease to be "limited" when applied to existing copyrights. . . . History reveals an unbroken congressional practice of granting to authors of works with existing copyrights the benefit of term extensions so that all under copyright protection will be governed evenhandedly under the same regime. . . .

Congress' consistent historical practice of applying newly enacted copyright terms to future and existing copyrights reflects a judgment stated concisely by Representative Huntington at the time of the 1831 Act: "[J]ustice, policy, and equity alike forb[id]" that an "author who had sold his [work] a week ago, be placed in a worse situation than the author who should sell his work the day after the passing of [the] act." The CTEA follows this historical practice by keeping the duration provisions of the 1976 Act largely in place and simply adding 20 years to each of them. Guided by text, history, and precedent, we cannot agree with petitioners' submission that extending the duration of existing copyrights is categorically beyond Congress' authority under the Copyright Clause.

Satisfied that the CTEA complies with the "limited times" prescription, we turn now to whether it is a rational exercise of the legislative authority conferred by the Copyright Clause. On that point we defer substantially to Congress.

The CTEA reflects judgments of a kind Congress typically makes—judgments we cannot dismiss as outside the Legislature's domain. . . . By extending the baseline United States copyright term to life plus 70 years, Congress sought to ensure that American authors would receive the same copyright protection in Europe as their European counterparts. The CTEA may also provide greater incentive for American and other authors to create and disseminate their work in the United States.

In addition to international concerns, Congress passed the CTEA in light of demographic, economic, and technological changes and rationally credited projections that longer terms would encourage copyright holders to invest in the restoration and public distribution of their works.

In sum, we find that the CTEA is a rational enactment; we are not at liberty to second-guess congressional determinations and policy judgments of this order, however debatable or arguably unwise they may be. Accordingly, we cannot conclude that the CTEA—which continues the unbroken congressional practice of treating future and existing copyrights in parity for term extension purposes—is an impermissible exercise of Congress' power under the Copyright Clause.

Unpersuasive Arguments

Petitioners' Copyright Clause arguments rely on several novel readings of the Clause. We next address these arguments and explain why we find them unpersuasive.

Petitioners contend that even if the CTEA's 20-year term extension is literally a "limited Tim[e]," permitting Congress to extend existing copyrights allows it to evade the "limited times" constraint by creating effectively perpetual copyrights through repeated extensions. We disagree.

As the Court of Appeals observed, a regime of perpetual copyrights "clearly is not the situation before us." Nothing before this Court warrants construction of the CTEA's 20-year term extension as a congressional attempt to evade or override the "limited times" constraint. Critically, we again emphasize, petitioners fail to show how the CTEA crosses a constitutionally significant threshold with respect to "limited times" that the 1831, 1909, and 1976 Acts did not. Those earlier Acts did not create perpetual copyrights and neither does the CTEA.

Petitioners dominantly advance a series of arguments all premised on the proposition that Congress may not extend an existing copyright absent new consideration from the author. They pursue this main theme under three headings. Petitioners contend that the CTEA's extension of existing copyrights (1) overlooks the requirement of "originality," (2) fails to "promote the Progress of Science," and (3) ignores copyright's *quid pro quo* ["this for that": something is given in return for benefits received].

Petitioners' "originality" argument draws on *Feist Publications, Inc. v. Rural Telephone Service Co.*[1] Relying on *Feist*, petitioners urge that even if a work is sufficiently "original" to qualify for copyright protection in the first instance, any extension of the copyright's duration is impermissible because, once published, a work is no longer original.

Feist, however, did not touch on the duration of copyright protection. Rather, the decision addressed the core question of copyrightability—*i.e.*, the "creative spark" a work must have to be eligible for copyright protection at all. Explaining the originality requirement, *Feist* trained on the Copyright Clause

---

1. When Feist Publications, Inc., copied information from Rural Telephone Service Company's telephone listings, the Supreme Court ruled the action constitutional in 1991 because the information is not copyrightable.

words "Authors" and "Writings." The decision did not construe the "limited times" for which a work may be protected, and the originality requirement has no bearing on that prescription.

CTEA Promotes Progress

More forcibly, petitioners contend that the CTEA's extension of existing copyrights does not "promote the Progress of Science," as contemplated by the preambular language of the Copyright Clause. To sustain this objection, petitioners do not argue that the Clause's preamble is an independently enforceable limit on Congress' power. Rather, they maintain that the preambular language identifies the sole end to which Congress may legislate; accordingly, they conclude, the meaning of "limited times" must be "determined in light of that specified end." The CTEA's extension of existing copyrights categorically fails to "promote the Progress of Science," petitioners argue, because it does not stimulate the creation of new works but merely adds value to works already created. . . .

We have . . . stressed, however, that it is generally for Congress, not the courts, to decide how best to pursue the Copyright Clause's objectives. The justifications we earlier set out for Congress' enactment of the CTEA provide a rational basis for the conclusion that the CTEA "promote[s] the Progress of Science."

On the issue of copyright duration, Congress from the start has routinely applied new definitions or adjustments of the copyright term to both future works and existing works not yet in the public domain. . . .

Congress' unbroken practice since the founding generation thus overwhelms petitioners' argument that the CTEA's extension of existing copyrights fails *per se* to "promote the Progress of Science."

Closely related to petitioners' preambular argument or a variant of it is their assertion that the Copyright Clause "imbeds a *quid pro quo*." They contend in this regard that Congress may grant to an "Autho[r]" an "exclusive Right" for a "limited Tim[e]," but only in exchange for a "Writin[g]." Congress' power to confer copyright protection, petitioners argue, is thus contingent upon an exchange: the author of an original work receives an "exclusive Right" for a "limited Tim[e]" in exchange for a dedication to the public thereafter. Extending an existing copyright without demanding additional consideration, petitioners maintain, bestows an unpaid-for benefit on copyright holders and their heirs in violation of the *quid pro quo* requirement.

We can demur to petitioners' description of the Copyright Clause as a grant of legislative authority empowering Congress "to secure a bargain—this for that." But the legislative evolution earlier recalled demonstrates what the bargain entails. Given the consistent placement of existing copyright holders in parity with future holders, the author of a work created in the last 170 years would reasonably comprehend, as the "this" offered her, a copyright not only for the time in place when protection is gained, but also for any renewal or extension legislated during that time. Congress could rationally seek to "promote . . . Progress" by including in every copyright statute an express guarantee that authors would receive the benefit of any later legislative extension of the copyright term. Nothing in the Copyright Clause bars Congress from creating the same incentive by adopting the same position as a matter of unbroken practice. . . .

For the several reasons stated, we find no Copyright Clause impediment to the CTEA's extension of existing copyrights.

Compatible with Free Speech

Petitioners separately argue that the CTEA is a content-neutral regulation of speech that fails heightened judicial review under the First Amendment. We reject petitioners' plea for imposition of uncommonly strict scrutiny on a copyright scheme that incorporates its own speech-protective purposes and safeguards. The Copyright Clause and First Amendment were adopted close in time. This proximity indicates that in the Framers' view, copyright's limited monopolies are compatible with free speech principles. Indeed, copyright's purpose is to *promote* the creation and publication of free expression. . . .

In addition to spurring the creation and publication of new expression, copyright law contains built-in First Amendment accommodations. First, it distinguishes between ideas and expression, and makes only the latter eligible for copyright protection. . . .

Due to this distinction, every idea, theory, and fact in a copyrighted work becomes instantly available for public exploitation at the moment of publication.

Second, the "fair use" defense allows the public to use not only facts and ideas contained in a copyrighted work, but also expression itself in certain circumstances. . . .

The fair use defense affords considerable "latitude for scholarship and comment" and even for parody ([e.g., a] rap group's musical parody of Roy Orbison's "Oh, Pretty Woman" may be fair use).

The CTEA itself supplements these traditional First Amendment safeguards. First, it allows libraries, archives, and similar institutions to "reproduce" and "distribute, display, or perform in facsimile or digital form" copies of certain published works "during the last 20 years of any term of copyright . . . for purposes of preservation, scholarship, or research" if the work is not already being exploited commercially and further copies are unavailable at a reasonable price. Second, Title II of the CTEA, known as the Fairness in Music Licensing Act of 1998, exempts small businesses, restaurants, and like entities from having to pay performance royalties on music played from licensed radio, television, and similar facilities.

Finally, the case petitioners principally rely upon for their First Amendment argument, *Turner Broadcasting System, Inc. v. FCC*, bears little on copyright. The statute at issue in *Turner* required cable operators to carry and transmit broadcast stations through their proprietary cable systems. Those "must carry" provisions, we explained, implicated "the heart of the First Amendment"—namely "the principle that each person should decide for himself or herself the ideas and beliefs deserving of expression, consideration, and adherence."

The CTEA, in contrast, does not oblige anyone to reproduce another's speech against the carrier's will. Instead, it protects authors' original expression from unrestricted exploitation. Protection of that order does not raise the free speech concerns present when the government compels or burdens the communication of particular facts or ideas. The First Amendment securely protects the freedom to make—or decline to make—one's own speech; it bears less heavily when speakers assert the right to make other people's speeches. To the extent such assertions raise First Amendment concerns, copyright's built-in free speech safeguards are generally adequate to address them. . . .

The Court Cannot Second-Guess Congress

If petitioners' vision of the Copyright Clause held sway, it would do more than render the CTEA's duration extensions unconstitutional as to existing works. Indeed, petitioners assertion that the provisions of the CTEA are not severable would make the CTEA's enlarged terms invalid even as to tomorrow's work. The 1976 Act's time extensions, which set the pattern that the CTEA followed, would be vulnerable as well.

As we read the Framers' instruction, the Copyright Clause empowers Congress to determine the intellectual property regimes that, overall, in that body's judgment, will serve the ends of the Clause. Beneath the facade of their inventive constitutional interpretation, petitioners forcefully urge that Congress pursued very bad policy in prescribing the CTEA's long terms. The wisdom of Congress' action, however, is not within our province to second-guess. Satisfied that the legislation before us remains inside the domain the Constitution assigns to the First Branch, we affirm the judgment of the Court of Appeals.

> *"With respect to films as with respect to other works, [copyright] extension does cause substantial harm to efforts to preserve and to disseminate works that were created long ago."*

Dissenting Opinion: The Copyright Term Extension Act Is Unconstitutional

Stephen Breyer

Stephen Breyer has served as a justice of the Supreme Court since 1994 and is the author of several books. He is known for an interpretation of law that emphasizes the purpose and consequences of the Constitution rather than its literal words. In the following dissenting opinion in Eldred v. Ashcroft, *he disagrees with the Court's ruling that Congress had the authority to pass the Copyright Term Extension Act (CTEA). In his opinion the CTEA is not justified by any objective expressed by the Copyright Clause of the Constitution. According to that clause, he says, the basic purpose of copyright is to promote knowledge and learning and to stimulate artistic creativity for the public good. Extending the term of existing copyrights will restrict the dissemination of knowledge by requiring royalties for use of older works and costly searches for permission, and will make it especially difficult to include them in electronic databases. It will not provide any incentive for creation of new works since the extended term will affect only corporations or the heirs of authors who have died. Justice Breyer does not see any way it will benefit*

Stephen Breyer, dissenting opinion, *Eldred v. Ashcroft*, U.S. Supreme Court, January 15, 2003.

the public and considers it unconstitutional because it is outside the scope of the power the Constitution grants to Congress.

The Copyright Clause and the First Amendment seek related objectives—the creation and dissemination of information. When working in tandem, these provisions mutually reinforce each other, the first serving as an "engine of free expression," the second assuring that government throws up no obstacle to its dissemination. At the same time, a particular statute that exceeds proper Copyright Clause bounds may set Clause and Amendment at cross-purposes, thereby depriving the public of the speech-related benefits that the Founders, through both, have promised.

Consequently, I would review plausible claims that a copyright statute seriously, and unjustifiably, restricts the dissemination of speech somewhat more carefully than reference to this Court's traditional Commerce Clause jurisprudence might suggest. . . . It is necessary only to recognize that this statute involves not pure economic regulation, but regulation of expression, and what may count as rational where economic regulation is at issue is not necessarily rational where we focus on expression—in a Nation constitutionally dedicated to the free dissemination of speech, information, learning, and culture. In this sense only, and where line-drawing among constitutional interests is at issue, I would look harder than does the majority at the statute's rationality—though less hard than precedent might justify.

Thus, I would find that the statute lacks the constitutionally necessary rational support (1) if the significant benefits that it bestows are private, not public; (2) if it threatens seriously to undermine the expressive values that the Copyright Clause embodies; and (3) if it cannot find justification in any significant Clause-related objective. Where, after examination of the statute, it becomes difficult, if not impossible, even to dispute these characterizations, Congress' "choice is clearly wrong."

Because we must examine the relevant statutory effects in light of the Copyright Clause's own purposes, we should begin by reviewing the basic objectives of that Clause. The Clause authorizes a "tax on readers for the purpose of giving a bounty to writers." Why? What constitutional purposes does the "bounty" serve?

The Constitution itself describes the basic Clause objective as one of "promot[ing] the Progress of Science," *i.e.*, knowledge and learning. The Clause exists not to "provide a special private benefit," but "to stimulate artistic creativity for the general public good." It does so by "motivat[ing] the creative activity of authors" through "the provision of a special reward." The "reward" is a means, not an end. And that is why the copyright term is limited. It is limited so that its beneficiaries—the public—"will not be permanently deprived of the fruits of an artist's labors. . . ."

Distribution of Classic Works

This statute, like virtually every copyright statute, imposes upon the public certain expression-related costs in the form of (1) royalties that may be higher than necessary to evoke creation of the relevant work, and (2) a requirement that one seeking to reproduce a copyrighted work must obtain the copyright holder's permission. The first of these costs translates into higher prices that will potentially restrict a work's dissemination. The second means search costs that themselves may prevent reproduction even where the author has no objection. Although these costs are, in a sense, inevitable concomitants of copyright protection, there are special reasons for thinking them especially serious here.

First, the present statute primarily benefits the holders of existing copyrights, *i.e.*, copyrights on works already created. And a Congressional Research Service (CRS) study prepared for Congress indicates that the added royalty-related sum that the law will transfer to existing copyright holders is large. In conjunction with official figures on copyright renewals, the CRS Report indicates that only about 2% of copyrights between 55 and 75 years old retain commercial value—*i.e.*, still generate royalties after that time. But books, songs, and movies of that vintage still earn about $400 million per year in royalties. Hence, (despite declining consumer interest in any given work over time) one might conservatively estimate that 20 extra years of copyright protection will mean the transfer of several billion extra royalty dollars to holders of existing copyrights—copyrights that, together, already will have earned many billions of dollars in royalty "reward."

The extra royalty payments will not come from thin air. Rather, they ultimately come from those who wish to read or see or hear those classic books or films or recordings that have survived. Even the $500,000 that United Airlines has had to pay for the right to play George Gershwin's 1924 classic *Rhapsody in Blue* represents a cost of doing business, potentially reflected in the ticket prices of those who fly. Further, the likely amounts of extra royalty payments are large enough to suggest that unnecessarily high prices will unnecessarily restrict distribution of classic works (or lead to disobedience of the law)—not just in theory but in practice.

Difficulty of Getting Permissions

A second, equally important, cause for concern arises out of the fact that copyright extension imposes a "permissions" requirement—not only upon potential users of "classic" works that still retain commercial value, but also upon potential users of *any other work* still in copyright. Again using CRS estimates, one can estimate that, by 2018, the number of such works 75 years of age or older will be about 350,000. Because the Copyright Act of 1976 abolished the requirement that an owner must renew a copyright, such "still in copyright" works (of little or no commercial value) will eventually number in the millions.

The potential users of such works include not only movie buffs and aging jazz fans, but also historians, scholars, teachers, writers, artists, database operators, and researchers of all kind—those who want to make the past accessible for their own use or for that of others. The permissions requirement can inhibit their ability to accomplish that task. Indeed, in an age where computer-accessible databases promise to facilitate research and learning, the permissions requirement can stand as a significant obstacle to realization of that technological hope.

The reason is that the permissions requirement can inhibit or prevent the use of old works (particularly those without commercial value): (1) because it may prove expensive to track down or to contract with the copyright holder, (2) because the holder may prove impossible to find, or (3) because the holder when found may deny permission either outright or through misinformed efforts to bargain. The CRS, for example, has found that the cost of seeking permission "can be prohibitive." . . .

To some extent costs of this kind accompany any copyright law, regardless of the length of the copyright term. But to extend that term, preventing works from the 1920's and 1930's from falling into the public domain, will dramatically increase the size of the costs just as—perversely—the likely benefits from protection diminish. The older the work, the less likely it retains commercial value, and the harder it will likely prove to find the current copyright holder. The older the work, the more likely it will prove useful to the historian, artist, or teacher. The older the work, the less likely it is that a sense of authors' rights can justify a copyright holder's decision not to permit reproduction, for the more likely it is that the copyright holder making the decision is not the work's creator, but, say, a corporation or a great-grandchild whom the work's creator never knew. Similarly, the costs of obtaining permission, now perhaps ranging in the millions of dollars, will multiply as the number of holders of affected copyrights increases from several hundred thousand to several million. The costs to the users of nonprofit databases, now numbering in the low millions, will multiply as the use of those computer-assisted databases becomes more prevalent. And the qualitative costs to education, learning, and research will multiply as our children become ever more dependent for the content of their knowledge upon computer-accessible databases—thereby condemning that which is not so accessible, say, the cultural content of early 20th-century history, to a kind of intellectual purgatory from which it will not easily emerge. . . .

The majority [of the Court] invokes the "fair use" exception, and it notes that copyright law itself is restricted to protection of a work's expression, not its substantive content. Neither the exception nor the restriction, however, would necessarily help those who wish to obtain from electronic databases material that is not there—say, teachers wishing their students to see albums of Depression Era photographs, to read the recorded words of those who actually lived under slavery, or to contrast, say, [actor] Gary Cooper's heroic portrayal of Sergeant York with filmed reality from the battlefield of Verdun. . . .

I should add that the Motion Picture Association of America also finds my concerns overstated at least with respect to films, because the extension will sometimes make it profitable to reissue old films, saving them from extinction. Other film preservationists note, however, that only a small minority of the many films, particularly silent films, from the 1920's and 1930's have been preserved. They seek to preserve the remainder. And they tell us that copyright extension will impede preservation by forbidding the reproduction of films within their own or within other public collections.

Because this subsection concerns only costs, not countervailing benefits, I shall simply note here that, with respect to films as with respect to other works, extension does cause substantial harm to efforts to preserve and to disseminate works that were created long ago. . . .

No Public Benefits

What copyright-related benefits might justify the statute's extension of copyright protection? First, no one could reasonably conclude that copyright's traditional economic rationale applies here. The extension will not act as an economic spur encouraging authors to create new works. No potential author can reasonably believe that he has more than a tiny chance of writing a classic that will survive commercially long enough for the copyright extension to matter. . . . And any remaining monetary incentive is diminished dramatically by the fact that the relevant royalties will not arrive until 75 years or more into the future, when, not the author, but distant heirs, or shareholders in a successor corporation, will receive them. . . .

What monetarily motivated [author of a potentially classic work] would not realize that he could do better for his grandchildren by putting a few dollars into an interest-bearing bank account? The Court itself finds no evidence to the contrary. It refers to testimony before Congress (1) that the copyright system's incentives encourage creation, and (2) that income earned from one work can help support an artist who "'continue[s] to create.'" But the first of these amounts to no more than a set of undeniably true propositions about the value of incentives in general. And the applicability of the second to this Act is mysterious. How will extension help today's Noah Webster [famed dictionary compiler] create new works 50 years after his death? Or is that hypothetical Webster supposed to support himself with the extension's present discounted value, *i.e.*, a few pennies? . . .

I am not certain why the Court considers it relevant in this respect that "[n]othing . . . warrants construction of the [1998 Act's] 20-year term extension as a congressional attempt to evade or override the 'limited times' constraint."

Of course Congress did not intend to act unconstitutionally. But it may have sought to test the Constitution's limits. After all, the statute was named after a Member of Congress [songwiter Sonny Bono], who, the legislative history records, "wanted the term of copyright protection to last forever." ...

Several publishers and film-makers argue that the statute provides incentives to *those who act as publishers* to republish and to redistribute older copyrighted works. This claim cannot justify this statute, however, because the rationale is inconsistent with the basic purpose of the Copyright Clause—as understood by the Framers and by this Court. The Clause assumes an initial grant of monopoly, designed primarily to encourage creation, followed by termination of the monopoly grant in order to promote dissemination of already-created works. It assumes that it is the *disappearance* of the monopoly grant, not its *perpetuation*, that will, on balance, promote the dissemination of works already in existence. This view of the Clause does not deny the empirical possibility that grant of a copyright monopoly to the heirs or successors of a long-dead author could *on occasion* help publishers resurrect the work, say, of a long-lost Shakespeare. But it does deny Congress the Copyright Clause power to base its actions primarily upon that empirical possibility—lest copyright grants become perpetual, lest on balance they restrict dissemination, lest too often they seek to bestow benefits that are solely retroactive. ...

Untrue to Copyright's Purpose

The statute's legislative history suggests another possible justification. That history refers frequently to the financial assistance the statute will bring the entertainment industry, particularly through the promotion of exports. I recognize that Congress has sometimes found that suppression of competition will help Americans sell abroad—though it has simultaneously taken care to protect American buyers from higher domestic prices. In doing so, however, Congress has exercised its commerce, not its copyright, power. I can find nothing in the Copyright Clause that would authorize Congress to enhance the copyright grant's monopoly power, likely leading to higher prices both at home and abroad, *solely* in order to produce higher foreign earnings. That objective is not a *copyright* objective. Nor, standing alone, is it related to any other objective more closely tied to the Clause itself. Neither can higher corporate profits alone justify the grant's enhancement. The Clause seeks public, not private, benefits.

Finally, the Court mentions as possible justifications "demographic, economic, and technological changes"—by which the Court apparently means the facts that today people communicate with the help of modern technology, live longer, and have children at a later age. The first fact seems to argue not for, but instead against, extension. The second fact seems already corrected for by the 1976 Act's life-plus-50 term, which automatically grows with lifespans. And the third fact—that adults are having children later in life—is a makeweight, at best, providing no explanation of why the 1976 Act's term of 50 years after an author's death—a longer term than was available to authors themselves for most of our Nation's history—is an insufficient potential bequest. The weakness of these final rationales simply underscores the conclusion that emerges from consideration of earlier attempts at justification: there is no legitimate serious copyright-related justification for this statute. . . .

I share the Court's initial concern about intrusion upon the decisionmaking authority of Congress. But I do not believe it intrudes upon that authority to find the statute unconstitutional on the basis of (1) a legal analysis of the Copyright Clause's objectives, (2) the total implausibility of any incentive effect, and (3) the statute's apparent failure to provide significant international uniformity. Nor does it intrude upon congressional authority to consider rationality in light of the expressive values underlying the Copyright Clause, related as it is to the First Amendment, and given the constitutional importance of correctly drawing the relevant Clause/Amendment boundary.... Vigilance is all the more necessary in a new Century that will see intellectual property rights and the forms of expression that underlie them play an ever more important role in the Nation's economy and the lives of its citizens....

This statute will cause serious expression-related harm. It will likely restrict traditional dissemination of copyrighted works. It will likely inhibit new forms of dissemination through the use of new technology. It threatens to interfere with efforts to preserve our Nation's historical and cultural heritage and efforts to use that heritage, say, to educate our Nation's children. It is easy to understand how the statute might benefit the private financial interests of corporations or heirs who own existing copyrights. But I cannot find any constitutionally legitimate copyright-related way in which the statute will benefit the public. Indeed, in respect to existing works, the serious public harm and the virtually nonexistent public benefit could not be more clear.

I have set forth the analysis upon which I rest these judgments. This analysis leads inexorably to the conclusion that the statute cannot be understood rationally to advance a constitutionally legitimate interest. The statute falls outside the scope of legislative power that the Copyright Clause, read in light of the First Amendment, grants to Congress. I would hold the statute unconstitutional.

> "Mr. Eldred is a striking example of how
> one person's efforts to advance scholar-
> ship and the public domain have been
> stifled by Congress's kowtowing to en-
> tertainment interests."

The Copyright Term
Extension Act Was Opposed
by Scholars and Libraries

Andrea L. Foster

Andrea L. Foster is a reporter for The Chronicle of Higher
Education. *In the following article she tells why Eric Eldred, who
was the plaintiff in* Eldred v. Ashcroft, *decided to challenge the
copyright extension law. Eldred was a retired computer expert
who loved books and who maintained a Web site at which he
posted the full texts of great literature. He believed it was important to make them available to new readers on the Internet. Of
course, he could not post copyrighted books, so he was able to
use only those on which the copyright had expired. It was due to
expire on several that he was looking forward to posting, but
Congress passed a law extending the copyrights on works until
long after their authors have died. Some people who believed this
was unfair to the public recruited Eldred to sue the government
on grounds that the new law was unconstitutional. He was supported by many scholarly groups such as library associations and
professors, and was opposed by large media companies that did
not want to lose the rights to older works.*

Eric Eldred is taking on the federal government in a [2003] U.S. Supreme Court showdown that pits him, scholars, and library groups against the nation's largest media companies. At issue is whether copyright policy can accommodate both the entertainment industry and consumers, who increasingly seek to gain access to movies, songs, and books over the Internet.

But here in this town of 34,000 [Derry, New Hampshire], where Scotch-Irish Presbyterians settled in 1719 to escape persecution, few people, apart from the local librarians, are aware of the high-profile court case, *Eldred v. Ashcroft*. Mr. Eldred, who has lived here for 25 years, is challenging the constitutionality of the Sonny Bono Copyright Term Extension Act, which added 20 years to copyright protection.

The 1998 act lengthened the copyrights on creative works to 70 years from 50 years after the creator's death. It protects works for hire for 95 years, up from 75 years.

"Am I supposed to know about him?" Chris Dornin, political reporter for the weekly *Derry News*, asks a visitor.

Eldred's Mission

That's just how Mr. Eldred wants it. At 59, he is unassuming, shy, and soft-spoken. Yet his passion for publishing on the Internet is unmistakable. He envisions a society in which literacy and democracy are advanced through the online dissemination and discussion of great literature.

Literature, he says, should not be "locked up in a library and accessible [only] to high priests of academia. . . . People have as much power as a printing press" in their own computers.

Harvard University's Berkman Center for Internet and Society, which spearheaded the lawsuit, approached Mr. Eldred after *The New York Times* ran an article in January 1999 about his struggle with copyright law. Jonathan L. Zittrain, a Harvard law professor who has helped craft the legal challenge—

along with the center's Lawrence Lessig and Charles R. Nesson—says Mr. Eldred is a striking example of how one person's efforts to advance scholarship and the public domain have been stifled by Congress's kowtowing to entertainment interests.

"You basically couldn't ask central casting for a better face," Mr. Zittrain says. "There's none of the sort of ego that one stereotypically encounters with people on a mission."

At the door of the 18th-century house he shares with his wife, Julie, Mr. Eldred is expressionless, with little to say. His face and gray hair are partly hidden by a Red Sox cap. Upstairs, lined floor to ceiling with books, he enters his home office. It is dark, musty, and also crowded with books, with a small space for a computer and scanner. He recommends a drive into town to talk at a diner or the library.

Working at home, Mr. Eldred, a former computer administrator, runs a Web site (http://www.eldritchpress.org) that makes great literature freely available. He has a fondness for [author Nathaniel] Hawthorne, although the works of many other writers, like [H.L.] Mencken, [Joseph] Conrad, and [Anton] Chekhov, are there, too, The site also features works about boats—he owns a 27-foot sloop—as well as a tribute to his mother, the late Bonnie Eldred, who was a poet and self-taught marine biologist.

"It mirrors him," says Mr. Zittrain. "It's clean and simple. This is not a site with pop-up ads and his name all over it."

Helping His Daughters

Mr. Eldred started the site in 1995, inspired to help his triplet daughters wade through the antique prose of [Hawthorne's] *The Scarlet Letter*, which they were assigned to read in middle school. Mr. Eldred's electronic text has hyperlinks throughout to explain difficult words and phrases. The site also includes links to color illustrations that accompanied a 1915 edition of the book.

His work on *The Scarlet Letter* motivated him to create a separate Web site on Hawthorne geared to high-school students and college undergraduates. It features a complete list of the author's works, readings about his life, criticism of his literature, correspondence with [Herman] Melville, and museums and libraries that maintain Hawthorne collections.

One page, "How to Get an 'A' on Your *Scarlet Letter* Assignment," admonishes students not to be "crybabies": Don't rely on Cliffs Notes or a movie adaptation of the book. Don't turn in someone else's work.

"We are trying to challenge you," Mr. Eldred writes. "Some of you students need to have older people ask you to do something hard, that you might fail at."

In October 1997, the National Endowment for the Humanities named the Hawthorne site one of the 20 best humanities sites on the World Wide Web.

"There's so much information on it. He's done a terrific job," says Leland S. Person, head of the English department at the University of Cincinnati and treasurer of the Nathaniel Hawthorne Society. Its Web site links to Mr. Eldred's.

Donna M. Campbell, an associate professor of English at Gonzaga University, praises Mr. Eldred's Web site on William Dean Howells. Mr. Eldred offered his Web postings on the author to the William Dean Howells Society, and they are now on the society's Web site. "He formatted the Howells novels beautifully," says Ms. Campbell. "He's been very, very important in terms of providing reliable online text. He explains where he got it and what he's done with it."

Mr. Eldred keeps track of the expiration dates of copyrights on American literary classics, so he can copy them to his site, using an Epson scanner and software with optical character recognition. He intended to republish *Horse and Men,* a short-story collection by Sherwood Anderson, and *New Hampshire,* a collection of Robert Frost poems. Both works, published in 1923, were set to enter the public domain in 1998 under the 75-year copyright protection in place before the Copyright Term Extension Act took effect.

The Sherwood Anderson Trust holds the rights to *Horses and Men*. It is unclear who holds the rights to *New Hampshire*.

Frost's farm is a tourist site in Derry, and Mr. Eldred says *New Hampshire* "has nice woodcuts that are not reproduced in later works." He wanted to republish *Horses and Men* without editors' punctuation changes in subsequent editions. "Taking out a comma changes the way a poem is read, a lot," says Mr. Eldred. "I'd rather leave that up to the reader than make those choices for them."

Dashed Plans

But his plans were dashed when Congress approved the Copyright Term Extension Act in early October 1998, which keeps the works out of the public domain for another 20 years. What's more, the House of Representatives that month approved the Digital Millennium Copyright Act, which barred people from circumventing technologies designed to restrict access to copyrighted works.

Mr. Eldred got mad. He fired off messages to the news media. He shut down his Web site for five days in protest and urged people to write to President [Bill] Clinton. The president signed both bills in late October.

The Copyright Term Extension Act, Mr. Eldred wrote in an Internet posting in November 1998, was "marginalizing the library, diminishing the public domain. . . . By allowing distant heirs and publishers with obsolete technology to maintain control, even the author's intent and original works may not be protected."

The act was named for the late Sonny Bono, an entertainer and, toward the end of his career, a member of the U.S. House of Representatives. Congress said the act would help authors and songwriters, like Mr. Bono. But Mr. Eldred argues that such creative people would still create their works without the extra 20 years of copyright protection.

It wasn't a good year for Mr. Eldred. He was forced to quit work as a computer-systems administrator because of numbness and pain in his arms, which kept him awake at night. A doctor diagnosed the problem as repetitive stress injury and recommended splints. That injured his thumbs, says Mr. Eldred. His chronic pain was later determined to be a symptom of thoracic outlet syndrome, in which the nerves of the upper body are compressed. He underwent physical therapy but couldn't return to work. He started receiving worker's-compensation benefits and, when they ended, Social Security disability payments.

He channeled his anger with Congress into action when the Berkman Center recruited him as the lead plaintiff in a lawsuit against then-Attorney General Janet Reno. The suit, filed in January 1999, asked the U.S. District Court for the District of Columbia to declare the Copyright Term Extension Act unconstitutional. Other plaintiffs included Dover Publications Inc., of Mineola, N.Y., which publishes paperback books, and Luck's Music Library Inc., of Madison Heights, Michigan, which sells and rents sheet music for classical works.

The suit argues that the act violates Article I, Section 8, of the U.S. Constitution, which grants Congress authority to confer copyrights for "limited times." By repeatedly extending copyrights—which originally were 14 years in length—Congress had failed to limit copyright protection, the plaintiffs said.

Copyright is intended to provide an incentive for artists and authors to create new works. But how can it, the lawyers ask, if copyright extensions apply retroactively, long after an author's death? Since, as a rule, people don't create works until they are at least adolescents, 95 years of copyright protection would seem necessary only if authors routinely lived well beyond 110 years, the suit points out. An amended complaint asserts that the act violates the First Amendment, because it restricts the ability to publish.

Judge June L. Green, of the district court, and, subsequently, the U.S. Court of Appeals for the District of Columbia Circuit, didn't buy the arguments. Congress has the authority to decide the meaning of "limited times" under the copyright clause of the Constitution, the judge said. The act does not violate the First Amendment, either, she said, because there is no First Amendment right to use the copyrighted works of others.

Challenging the Government

Mr. Eldred's legal challenge may seem like an audacious act for a quiet bookworm. But, in fact, he has been challenging the government for years.

After graduating from Harvard with a major in philosophy in 1966, he became active in Students for a Democratic Society. He once spent the night in jail for blocking the entrance of a Boston hospital to protest what he and the radical group considered its racist policies. As a member of the Boston Draft Resistance Group, he boarded buses with draftees headed for physical exams and tried to persuade them that it would be wrong for them to fight in the Vietnam War.

He was drafted to serve in the war but won conscientious-objector status and went to work as a respiratory therapist at Massachusetts General Hospital. Later he was promoted to chief pulmonary technologist and managed a laboratory. He also became the resident computer expert for many physicians. He went on to work as a computer consultant and supervisor at several software and publishing companies.

Mr. Eldred's Web site displays his skepticism of authority. Before the arrest of Theodore J. Kaczynski, in 1996, government officials had said that the Unabomber might have drawn inspiration for his acts from Conrad's novel *The Secret Agent* "I thought it was absurd," says Mr. Eldred, noting that Conrad wrote with irony about the anarchist leanings of Verlac, the character who sets about bombing an observatory. So Mr. Eldred posted the text of the work on his site, along with an article from *The Washington Post* on the government's theory.

Although in court he is fighting only the latest extension of copyright, Mr. Eldred really wants copyright policy completely overhauled, to favor consumers over creators. Creative works, he says, should become part of the public domain unless the creators deliberately copyright them. Under current law, a work is copyrighted automatically upon its creation. He also says it may be desirable for literature to be copyrighted for only 14 years—as it was at first, in 1790—with authors permitted to renew the copyright for another 14 years.

He struggled over whether to appeal the case to the Supreme Court, seeking advice from a community of online publishers called the "book people." They share ideas through an e-mail list about disseminating and preserving literature and scanning books into computers. The group took its name from *Fahrenheit 451*, the Ray Bradbury novel about a society in which all books are burned because they're seen as upsetting the status quo. A secretive network of "book people" emerges to preserve works of literature by memorizing them.

Support from Scholars

Mr. Eldred was wary of an appeal because he was afraid that the Supreme Court justices would issue a ruling that not only agreed with the government but also strongly affirmed the notion that copyrights are akin to natural property rights. "Is that not worse off than leaving the matter ambiguous?" he asked his compatriots.

Their response was indeterminate, and he decided to take the risk, along with the other plaintiffs. Surprisingly, the justices agreed to hear the case. The Supreme Court usually accepts a case only when lower courts disagree in their decisions.

Scholarly groups came out in full force for Mr. Eldred, filing about a dozen legal briefs in support of his lawsuit. His supporters include 15 library associations, 5 professors of constitutional law, 53 professors of intellectual-property law, 17 economists, and various academic-affiliated groups, including the College Art Association, and the Consortium of College and University Media Centers, and the National Humanities Alliance.

Their legal briefs said the Copyright Term Extension Act grants copyright holders too much control over the dissemination of creative works, constraining the ability of scholars and teachers to discuss and study literature, art, and movies.

On the other side, the government's side attracted copyright holders like AOL Time Warner Inc., the Association of American Publishers, Dr. Seuss Enterprises, the Motion Picture Association of America, and the Recording Industry Association of America. Their briefs argue that the Constitution leaves it up to Congress to decide whether to extend copyrights, that the 1998 act makes U.S. copyright law more harmonious with Europe's, and that applying copyright safeguards to existing works encourages copyright holders to restore and disseminate their works.

After going before the Supreme Court [in October 2002], Mr. Lessig, who argued Mr. Eldred's case, spoke to reporters on the front steps of the court building. When he finished, reporters asked for Mr. Eldred. After a brief search, he was found talking to Mr. Lessig's parents and was pulled aside to answer reporters' questions.

Mr. Eldred had similarly tried to stay in the background at a party for him and his legal team on the eve of the arguments before the Supreme Court. Hardly anyone noticed when the plaintiff, wearing his Red Sox cap, entered the room. When Mr. Lessig entered, the crowd fell silent to allow him to speak. And Mr. Eldred, like a concerned parent, told him to go home and get some sleep.

For online publishing to have a chance to flourish, Mr. Eldred knew, his lawyer would have to be fully alert the next morning.

"My focus is on discovering and trying to help other people with the tools to be able to do this themselves," he says, "rather than relying on a university or a professor or anybody else to give this to them."

> *"Critics blasted the new law as "the Mickey Mouse Protection Act" and complained that consumers would be forced to pay hundreds of millions of dollars for access to creative works that rightfully belong to them."*

The Copyright Term Extension Act Does Not Serve the Purpose of Copyright

David Bollier

David Bollier, journalist and public policy analyst, is a senior fellow at the University of Southern California Annenberg School for Communications. In the following excerpt from his book Brand Name Bullies, *he explains why he thinks the Copyright Term Extension Act is not in the public interest. He argues that it does not serve the purpose of copyright, which is to provide a financial incentive to authors to create new works. Extending the term of copyright, he contends, benefits only dead authors or their estates, and therefore cannot encourage the creation of anything new. It is merely a giveaway to large media corporations such as the Walt Disney Company, which lobbied for the law to prevent the copyright on Mickey Mouse from expiring. In Bollier's opinion, the Supreme Court made the wrong decision about the case. He criticizes the Court for deferring to Congress and not stating any way in which copyright extension benefits the public. He maintains, however, that the case has raised public con-*

David Bollier, *Brand Name Bullies: The Quest to Control and Own Culture.* John Wiley & Sons, Inc., 2005, pp. 148–152. Copyright © 2005 by David Bollier. This material is used by permission of John Wiley & Sons, Inc.

sciousness in regard to the issue and has led to an increase in acts of civil disobedience against what he considers antisocial aspects of copyright law.

Like most Americans, Eric Eldred, a retired Navy computer contractor, thought that the vast universe of novels, short stories, and poems that are in the public domain belongs to everyone. That was before the Disney Company and other major media corporations decided they wanted to keep large swaths of American artistry for themselves, enlisting Congress to authorize their culture grab.

The story starts in 1995, the dawn of mass usage of the Internet. Eldred's teenaged daughters had received a school assignment to read a classic of American literature, Nathaniel Hawthorne's *The Scarlet Letter.* Eldred decided to explore how the Internet might be able to make the book more interesting and accessible. After creating his own Web version of the book using a contemporary font, he added annotations to the text, a glossary of archaic words, Web links to other works by Hawthorne, and reviews of the book from the 1870s, when it was first published.

Excited by the outcome, Eldred set about expanding his project. Within a few years, he had created online versions of literature by Henry James, Oliver Wendell Holmes, Wallace Stevens, Willa Cather, and hundreds of other great American authors. Since the copyrights on all of the works had expired, Eldred could do whatever he wanted with the texts. Soon his innovative Web site was receiving 20,000 hits a day. The National Endowment for the Humanities cited it as one of the twenty best humanities sites on the Web.

In 1998, however, Congress, acting at the behest of the Disney Company, sideswiped Eldred's grand experiment. An early cartoon version of Mickey Mouse, as depicted in the 1928 cartoon short "Steamboat Willie," was due to enter the public domain in 2004. Pluto, Goofy, and Donald Duck were due to become public property in 2009. To protect its lucrative characters, Disney instigated an aggressive lobbying campaign to extend copyright terms of existing works by twenty years. It sweetened its case by giving contributions to eighteen of the twenty-five congressional sponsors of the legislation.

Besides protecting Disney characters, the bill—the Sonny Bono Copyright Term Extension Act—would also lock up an estimated 400,000 books, movies, and songs due to enter the public domain in 1998 and following years. Instead of becoming available to the public for free, as long anticipated, these works would be owned and controlled by private parties until at least 2018.

Incentive to Create New Works

A key rationale for copyright protection is the need to give authors a financial incentive to create new works. Unless artists have exclusive property rights in their writing, music, and films, they will not be able to sell them in the marketplace and earn a livelihood. It is a reasonable argument. Copyright scholars and content industries have long argued that copyright is a needed incentive to creative output.

But here Congress was giving a lucrative new financial incentive to *dead authors* who would never generate new creative works in return. The new monopoly rights were not going to stimulate George Gershwin, Joseph Conrad, Robert Frost, Lewis Carroll, Cole Porter, Sherwood Anderson, or F. Scott Fitzgerald to produce new masterpieces. The term extension amounted to a pure government giveaway to large media corporations and authors' estates. Critics blasted the new law as "the Mickey Mouse Protection Act" and complained that consumers would be forced to pay hundreds of millions of dollars for access to creative works that rightfully belong to them. The lockup of works was especially perverse because it was coming just as new technologies, especially the Internet, were providing the means for broader, easier public access to public-domain works.

Critics also noted the stunning inefficiency of the law. Only about 2 percent of works from the 1920s and 1930s generate any commercial revenues today. Yet the law would also restrict public access to the remaining 98 percent of works that have no apparent commercial value. Anyone wishing to use those works would find it extremely difficult to do so because of the notorious complications and expense of identifying rights-holders and negotiating licensing fees.

These arguments hardly mattered, and indeed, hardly registered. Congress enacted the Sonny Bono Copyright Term Extension Act, with virtually no debate, on October 2, 1998.

When Lawrence Lessig, then a professor at Harvard Law School, learned that the new law had forced Eric Eldred to shut down his Web site, he decided that the law was not just bad public policy, but unconstitutional. He pointed out that the Constitution, in Article I, Section 8, clearly stipulates that Congress is authorized to grant copyrights "for limited times" in order "to promote the progress of science and useful arts." The law met neither of these conditions, he argued.

While ostensibly limited, the terms of copyright protection have been extended so many times over the past two hundred years—eleven times since 1960—that the law scholar Peter Jaszi has called it "perpetual copyright on the installment plan." The first copyright law, enacted in 1790, was for a fourteen-year term, later made renewable for another fourteen years. Congress extended copyright terms so many times over the next two centuries that by 1998 copyrights for individuals lasted for the lifetime of the author plus seventy years, and for corporate copyright holders, ninety-five years. These periods of time are presumed to be necessary for authors to be sufficiently rewarded to produce what they do.

For copyright maximalists, even these generous terms were not enough. Sonny Bono's widow, Mary Bono, who succeeded her husband as a member of Congress, declared that "copyright should be forever." Jack Valenti, the film industry's top lobbyist, in shrewd deference to the Constitution's "limited times" clause, conceded he would be happy if copyright terms lasted "forever minus a day."

Was Extension Unconstitutional?

Determined to strike down the law as unconstitutional, Professor Lessig initiated a federal lawsuit on Eldred's behalf in January 1999. While some legal scholars considered the case a bit daffy—no one had ever questioned the constitutionality of copyright terms before—other legal experts rallied to the cause and helped Lessig frame his case. In October 1999, a federal district court upheld Congress's authority to extend copyright terms. This ruling was later upheld by the U.S. Circuit Court of Appeals, by a 2-to-1 margin.

It was something of a surprise, therefore, when the U.S. Supreme Court, in February 2002, agreed to review the case, *Eldred v. Ashcroft.* By now, the once-obscure topic of copyright terms was attracting a groundswell of public attention. The press began to explore the public's stake in copyright law. Lessig and Valenti engaged in showy debates. Eldred's brief to the Supreme Court was supported by some thirty-eight friend-of-the-court briefs submitted by such allies as Public Knowledge, the Electronic Frontier Foundation, the Free Software Foundation, Phyllis Schafly's Eagle Forum, the Intel Corporation, and a group of major economists that included Milton Friedman and Kenneth Arrow.

When the case was argued before the court in October 2002, none of the justices had positive things to say about the Copyright Term Extension Act. Justice Sandra Day O'Connor put it bluntly: "It is hard to understand, if the overall purpose of the Copyright Clause is to encourage creative work, how some retroactive extension could possibly do that." Yet the justices were wary that the court could specify an appropriate term limit for copyrights; they suggested that this is a classic legislative matter.

In January 2003, the Supreme Court upheld the constitutionality of the copyright term extension on precisely this ground. Writing for the 7-to-2 majority, Justice Ruth Bader Ginsburg said, "We are not at liberty to second-guess Congressional determinations and policy judgments of this order, however debatable or arguably unwise they may be." The court noted that Congress had, on other occasions, extended the duration of existing copyrights when extending the duration of copyrights for future works. The 1998 term extension was no different in kind, the court held.

Negative Reaction to Decision

In the wake of the decision, one copyright commentator likened it to the "Dred Scott case [a landmark case that was wrongly decided] for culture." Justice Ginsburg had rejected the idea that copyright is a bargain with the American people, and had not even addressed how the act promoted the progress of science and the useful arts. The ruling also seemed to signal that the courts were not likely to consider the constitutional dimensions of copyright law, but to defer to Congress instead.

One bright spot in Ginsburg's ruling was her strong affirmation of the "fair use doctrine," which allows the public to use portions of copyrighted works for personal, educational, and noncommercial purposes. But her confidence in the actual vitality of fair use—in the face of court rulings and new technologies that are nullifying those rights—seemed more rhetorical than convincing.

In a forceful dissent, Justice Stephen Breyer found no identifiable benefit to the public from the law. He also pointed out that authors will not benefit from the ruling, only "their heirs, estates or corporate successors." In short, authors and the public are getting screwed again.

In many ways, however, the *Eldred* case represented more of a beginning than an ending, and more of a rallying cry than an elegy. The day after the Supreme Court's ruling, the *New York Times* headline read, "A Corporate Victory, But One That Raises Public Consciousness." Acts of civil disobedience against the antisocial, personally intrusive claims of copyright law have only grown since the *Eldred* ruling, in part because of it.

CHAPTER 4

Distributing Software Intended for Illegal File-Sharing Violates Copyright Law

Case Overview

Metro-Goldwyn-Mayer Studios, Inc. v. Grokster, Ltd. (2005)

The illegal downloading of copyrighted files from the Internet—especially music and movie files—is an ever-increasing problem for copyright holders. Though in some cases, people who download such files have been caught and sued, it is impossible to catch more than a small fraction of them. Therefore, the entertainment industry has turned to suing the distributors of software that facilitates illegal file sharing.

The first and most famous case of this kind was *A & M Records v. Napster*, which was decided in 2001. Napster, an early file-sharing service, was so popular that it overloaded college networks with music-file transfers, causing some colleges to block it. When a court ordered it to take steps to prevent the sharing of copyrighted music, it could not do it and was shut down. However, other file-sharing services soon arose in its place. Prominent among these was Grokster.

Grokster, unlike Napster—which had stored files on its own server—was a peer-to-peer (P2P) network that used technology through which files were sent directly from one user's computer to another. A similar company, StreamCast, distributed equivalent software. These companies believed that because they neither stored illegal files nor could determine who downloaded them, and because their software could also be used for legal purposes, they would not be liable for copyright infringement. However, they were sued by a group of movie studios, recording companies, songwriters, and music publishers. (Though only Metro Goldwyn Mayer and Grokster were named in the case title, others in the group were parties to it, and so was StreamCast, another file-sharing service.) The lower courts held, on the basis of a rule set by an earlier Supreme Court decision, *Sony v. Universal Studios* (see chapter 1 of this book), that the legal uses of the software made the services immune to liability. The case was then appealed to the Supreme Court.

The central issue in the Supreme Court case was whether the *Sony* rule applied in this case. The circuit court had ruled that it did, but the two cases were different in many respects. Sony, which produced VCRs, had not encouraged illegal copying of TV shows; it had emphasized time-shifting in its advertising, and the Court had decided that time-shifting was legal. Grokster and StreamCast, on the other hand, had deliberately promoted their services as a replacement for Napster. An internal e-mail from a company executive stated: "We have put this network in place so that when Napster pulls the plug on their free service . . . or if the Court orders them shut down prior to that . . . we will be positioned to capture the flood of their 32 million users that will be actively looking for an alternative."

Although they had no specific knowledge of who had downloaded copyrighted files, Grokster and StreamCast not only were aware that many people were doing so, but had publicized the availability of such files. And their aim had been to make money; whereas their software was free to users, they sold advertising based on how many users they could attract and how many downloads were made. Therefore, the Court decided unanimously that inducing people to break the law makes a company liable to suit, even when the company itself has not broken the law. (Though this decision was unanimous, some of the justices felt that it did not go far enough, and wrote, or signed, concurring opinions expressing their own views.)

Grokster was shut down after the case was settled. Many sites now exist where copyrighted songs can be downloaded legally for a small fee. But illegal file sharing continues, and so far no way has been found to stop it.

> "One who distributes a device with the object of promoting its use to infringe copyright ... is liable for the resulting acts of infringement by third parties."

Unanimous Opinion: Companies That Encourage Illegal File-Sharing Are Liable for Copyright Infringement

David Souter

David Souter has been a justice of the Supreme Court since 1990. Although he was thought to be a conservative when he was appointed, he generally votes with the Court's liberal wing. The following opinion presents the Court's unanimous decision in the case of MGM v. Grokster, *ruling that Grokster and another company, StreamCast, which distributed peer-to-peer (P2P) file-sharing software, could be sued for copyright infringement even though they did not store any illegal files on their own servers. The circuit court had held that they were not liable because* Sony v. Universal Studios *had established the principle that producers of technology that is used illegally cannot be sued as long as their products also have legal uses. However, Justice Souter says, that does not apply when companies actively encourage illegal downloading and promote their software for that purpose, as Grokster and StreamCast did. The fact that they had no way of knowing which users had downloaded copyrighted files from other users does not matter, since they clearly intended to profit from third-party copyright infringement.*

David Souter, lead opinion, *Metro-Goldwyn-Mayer Studios v. Grokster*, U.S. Supreme Court, June 27, 2005.

The question is under what circumstances the distributor of a product capable of both lawful and unlawful use is liable for acts of copyright infringement by third parties using the product. We hold that one who distributes a device with the object of promoting its use to infringe copyright, as shown by clear expression or other affirmative steps taken to foster infringement, is liable for the resulting acts of infringement by third parties. . . .

MGM's [Metro-Goldwyn-Mayer Studios] evidence gives reason to think that the vast majority of [Grokster] users' downloads are acts of infringement, and because well over 100 million copies of the software in question are known to have been downloaded, and billions of files are shared across the FastTrack [technology used by Grokster] and Gnutella [technology used by Streamcast] networks each month, the probable scope of copyright infringement is staggering.

Grokster and StreamCast concede the infringement in most downloads, and it is uncontested that they are aware that users employ their software primarily to download copyrighted files, even if the decentralized FastTrack and Gnutella networks fail to reveal which files are being copied, and when. From time to time, moreover, the companies have learned about their users' infringement directly, as from users who have sent email to each company with questions about playing copyrighted movies they had downloaded, to whom the companies have responded with guidance. And MGM notified the companies of 8 million copyrighted files that could be obtained using their software.

Grokster and StreamCast are not, however, merely passive recipients of information about infringing use. The record is replete with evidence that from the moment Grokster and StreamCast began to distribute their free software, each one clearly voiced the objective that recipients use it to download copyrighted works, and each took active steps to encourage infringement.

After the notorious file-sharing service Napster was sued by copyright holders for facilitation of copyright infringement, StreamCast gave away a software program of a kind known as OpenNap, designed as compatible with the Napster program and open to Napster users for downloading files from other Napster and OpenNap users' computers. . . .

StreamCast developed promotional materials to market its service as the best Napster alternative. One proposed advertisement read: "Napster Inc. has announced that it will soon begin charging you a fee. That's if the courts don't order it shut down first. What will you do to get around it?" . . .

Attracting Infringers

StreamCast's executives monitored the number of songs by certain commercial artists available on their networks, and an internal communication indicates they aimed to have a larger number of copyrighted songs available on their networks than other file-sharing networks. The point, of course, would be to attract users of a mind to infringe, just as it would be with their promotional materials developed showing copyrighted songs as examples of the kinds of files available through Morpheus [software used by StreamCast]. Morpheus in fact allowed users to search specifically for "Top 40" songs, which were inevitably copyrighted. Similarly, Grokster sent users a newsletter promoting its ability to provide particular, popular copyrighted materials.

In addition to this evidence of express promotion, marketing, and intent to promote further, the business models employed by Grokster and StreamCast confirm that their principal object was use of their software to download copyrighted works. Grokster and StreamCast receive no revenue from users, who obtain the software itself for nothing. Instead, both companies generate income by selling advertising space, and they stream the advertising to Grokster and Morpheus users while they are employing the programs. As the number of users of each program increases, advertising opportunities become worth more. While there is doubtless some demand for free Shakespeare, the evidence shows that substantive volume is a function of free access to copyrighted work. Users seeking Top 40 songs, for example, or the latest release by Modest Mouse, are certain to be far more numerous than those seeking a free *Decameron* [a literary classic from the Italian Renaissance] and Grokster and StreamCast translated that demand into dollars.

Finally, there is no evidence that either company made an effort to filter copyrighted material from users' downloads or otherwise impede the sharing of copyrighted files. Although Grokster appears to have sent emails warning users about infringing content when it received threatening notice from the copyright holders, it never blocked anyone from continuing to use its software to share copyrighted files. StreamCast not only rejected another company's offer of help to monitor infringement, but blocked the Internet Protocol addresses of entities it believed were trying to engage in such monitoring on its networks. . . .

Managing the Tradeoff

MGM and many of the *amici* [friends of the court] fault the Court of Appeals' holding for upsetting a sound balance between the respective values of supporting creative pursuits through copyright protection and promoting innovation in new communication technologies by limiting the incidence of liability for copyright infringement. The more artistic protection is favored, the more technological innovation may be discouraged; the administration of copyright law is an exercise in managing the tradeoff.

The tension between the two values is the subject of this case, with its claim that digital distribution of copyrighted material threatens copyright holders as never before, because every copy is identical to the original, copying is easy, and many people (especially the young) use file-sharing software to download copyrighted works. This very breadth of the software's use may well draw the public directly into the debate over copyright policy, and the indications are that the ease of copying songs or movies using software like Grokster's and Napster's is fostering disdain for copyright protection. As the case has been presented to us, these fears are said to be offset by the different concern that imposing liability not only on infringers, but on distributors of software based on its potential for unlawful use, could limit further development of beneficial technologies.

The argument for imposing indirect liability in this case is, however, a powerful one given the number of infringing downloads that occur every day using StreamCast's and Grokster's software. When a widely shared service or product is used to commit infringement, it may be impossible to enforce rights in the protected work effectively against all direct infringers, the only practical alternative being to go against the distributor of the copying device for secondary liability on a theory of contributory or vicarious infringement. . . .

This Court has dealt with secondary copyright infringement in only one recent case, and because MGM has tailored its principal claim to our opinion there, a look at our earlier holding is in order. In *Sony Corp. v. Universal City Studios*, this Court addressed a claim that secondary liability for infringement can arise from the very distribution of a commercial product. There, the product, novel at the time, was what we know today as the videocassette recorder or VCR. Copyright holders sued Sony as the manufacturer, claiming it was contributorily liable for infringement that occurred when VCR owners taped copyrighted programs because it supplied the means used to infringe, and it had constructive knowledge that infringement would occur. At the trial on the merits, the evidence showed that the principal use of the VCR was for "'time-shifting,'" or taping a program for later viewing at a more convenient time, which the Court found to be a fair, not an infringing, use. There was no evidence that Sony had expressed an object of bringing about taping in violation of copyright or had taken active steps to increase its profits from unlawful taping. Although Sony's advertisements urged consumers to buy the VCR to "'record favorite shows'" or "'build a library'" of recorded programs, neither of these uses was necessarily infringing.

On those facts, with no evidence of stated or indicated intent to promote infringing uses, the only conceivable basis for imposing liability was on a theory of contributory infringement arising from its sale of VCRs to consumers with knowledge that some would use them to infringe. But because the VCR was "capable of commercially significant noninfringing uses," we held the manufacturer could not be faulted solely on the basis of its distribution. . . .

The *Sony* Rule v. the Inducement Rule

The parties and many of the *amici* in this case think the key to resolving it is the *Sony* rule and, in particular, what it means for a product to be "capable of commercially significant noninfringing uses." MGM advances the argument that granting summary judgment to Grokster and StreamCast as to their current activities gave too much weight to the value of innovative technology, and too little to the copyrights infringed by users of their software, given that 90% of works available on one of the networks was shown to be copyrighted. Assuming the remaining 10% to be its noninfringing use, MGM says this should not qualify as "substantial," and the Court should quantify *Sony* to the extent of holding that a product used "principally" for infringement does not qualify. As mentioned before, Grokster and StreamCast reply by citing evidence that their software can be used to reproduce public domain works, and they point to copyright holders who actually encourage copying. Even if infringement is the principal practice with their software today, they argue, the noninfring-ing uses are significant and will grow.

We agree with MGM that the Court of Appeals misapplied *Sony,* which it read as limiting secondary liability quite be-yond the circumstances to which the case applied.... The Ninth Circuit has read *Sony's* limitation to mean that when-ever a product is capable of substantial lawful use, the pro-ducer can never be held contributorily liable for third parties' infringing use of it; it read the rule as being this broad, even when an actual purpose to cause infringing use is shown by evidence independent of design and distribution of the prod-uct, unless the distributors had "specific knowledge of in-fringement at a time at which they contributed to the in-fringement, and failed to act upon that information." Because the Circuit found the StreamCast and Grokster software ca-pable of substantial lawful use, it concluded on the basis of its reading of *Sony* that neither company could be held liable, since there was no showing that their software, being without any central server, afforded them knowledge of specific unlaw-ful uses....

Sony's rule limits imputing culpable intent as a matter of law from the characteristics or uses of a distributed product. But nothing in *Sony* requires courts to ignore evidence of in-tent if there is such evidence, and the case was never meant to foreclose rules of fault-based liability derived from the com-mon law. Thus, where evidence goes beyond a product's char-acteristics or the knowledge that it may be put to infringing uses, and shows statements or actions directed to promoting infringement, *Sony's* staple-article rule will not preclude liability....

For the same reasons that *Sony* took the staple-article doc-trine of patent law as a model for its copyright safe harbor rule, the inducement rule, too, is a sensible one for copyright. We adopt it here, holding that one who distributes a device with the object of promoting its use to infringe copyright, as shown by clear expression or other affirmative steps taken to foster infringement, is liable for the resulting acts of infringement by third parties. We are, of course, mindful of the need to keep from trenching on regular commerce or discouraging the development of technologies with lawful and unlawful potential. Accordingly, just as *Sony* did not find intentional inducement despite the knowledge of the VCR manufacturer that its device could be used to infringe, mere knowledge of infringing potential or of actual infringing uses would not be enough here to subject a distributor to liability. Nor would ordinary acts incident to product distribution, such as offering customers technical support or product updates, support liability in themselves. The inducement rule, instead, premises liability on purposeful, culpable expression and conduct, and thus does nothing to compromise legitimate commerce or discourage innovation having a lawful promise. . . .

Napster Case More Important

The classic instance of inducement is by advertisement or solicitation that broadcasts a message designed to stimulate others to commit violations. MGM claims that such a message is shown here. It is undisputed that StreamCast beamed onto the computer screens of users of Napster-compatible programs ads urging the adoption of its OpenNap program, which was designed, as its name implied, to invite the custom of patrons of Napster, then under attack in the courts for facilitating massive infringement. Those who accepted StreamCast's OpenNap program were offered software to perform the same services, which a factfinder could conclude would readily have been understood in the Napster market as the ability to download copyrighted music files. Grokster distributed an electronic newsletter containing links to articles promoting its software's ability to access popular copyrighted music. And anyone whose Napster or free file-sharing searches turned up a link to Grokster would have understood Grokster to be offering the same file-sharing ability as Napster, and to the same people who probably used Napster for infringing downloads; that would also have been the understanding of anyone offered Grokster's suggestively named Swaptor software, its version of OpenNap. And both companies communicated a clear message by responding affirmatively to requests for help in locating and playing copyrighted materials.

In StreamCast's case, of course, the evidence just described was supplemented by other unequivocal indications of unlawful purpose in the internal communications and advertising designs aimed at Napster users. . . . The summary judgment record is replete with other evidence that Grokster and Stream-Cast, unlike the manufacturer and distributor in *Sony*, acted with a purpose to cause copyright violations by use of software suitable for illegal use.

Three features of this evidence of intent are particularly notable. First, each company showed itself to be aiming to satisfy a known source of demand for copyright infringement, the market comprising former Napster users. StreamCast's internal documents made constant reference to Napster, it initially distributed its Morpheus software through an OpenNap program compatible with Napster, it advertised its OpenNap program to Napster users, and its Morpheus software functions as Napster did except that it could be used to distribute more kinds of files, including copyrighted movies and software programs. Grokster's name is apparently derived from Napster, it too initially offered an OpenNap program, its software's function is likewise comparable to Napster's, and it attempted to divert queries for Napster onto its own Web site. Grokster and StreamCast's efforts to supply services to former Napster users, deprived of a mechanism to copy and distribute what were overwhelmingly infringing files, indicate a principal, if not exclusive, intent on the part of each to bring about infringement.

Second, this evidence of unlawful objective is given added significance by MGM's showing that neither company attempted to develop filtering tools or other mechanisms to diminish the infringing activity using their software. While the Ninth Circuit treated the defendants' failure to develop such tools as irrelevant because they lacked an independent duty to monitor their users' activity, we think this evidence underscores Grokster's and StreamCast's intentional facilitation of their users' infringement.

Third, there is a further complement to the direct evidence of unlawful objective. It is useful to recall that StreamCast and Grokster make money by selling advertising space, by directing ads to the screens of computers employing their software. As the record shows, the more the software is used, the more ads are sent out and the greater the advertising revenue becomes. Since the extent of the software's use determines the gain to the distributors, the commercial sense of their enterprise turns on high-volume use, which the record shows is infringing. This evidence alone would not justify an inference of unlawful intent, but viewed in the context of the entire record its import is clear.

The unlawful objective is unmistakable.

In addition to intent to bring about infringement and distribution of a device suitable for infringing use, the inducement theory of course requires evidence of actual infringement by recipients of the device, the software in this case. As the account of the facts indicates, there is evidence of infringement on a gigantic scale, and there is no serious issue of the adequacy of MGM's showing on this point in order to survive the companies' summary judgment requests. Although an exact calculation of infringing use as a basis for a claim of damages is subject to dispute, there is no question that the summary judgment evidence is at least adequate to entitle MGM to go forward with claims for damages and equitable relief.

In sum, this case is significantly different from *Sony*, and reliance on that case to rule in favor of StreamCast and Grokster was [an] error. *Sony* dealt with a claim of liability based solely on distributing a product with alternative lawful and unlawful uses with knowledge that some users would follow the unlawful course. The case struck a balance between the interests of protection and innovation by holding that the product's capability of substantial lawful employment should bar the imputation of fault and consequent secondary liability for the unlawful acts of others.

MGM's evidence in this case most obviously addresses a different basis of liability for distributing a product open to alternative uses. Here, evidence of the distributors' words and deeds going beyond distribution as such shows a purpose to cause and profit from third-party acts of copyright infringement. If liability for inducing infringement is ultimately found, it will not be on the basis of presuming or imputing fault, but from inferring a patently illegal objective from statements and actions showing what that objective was.

> *"Millions of songwriters, screenwriters, artists, technicians, recording engineers, movie technicians and others are the individual victims of this massive, ongoing theft."*

File-Sharing Networks Hurt Artists and Discourage the Creation of New Works

Richard K. Armey

Richard K. Armey, a former House majority leader in Congress, is cochairman of the conservative nonprofit organization Freedom Works. In the following commentary on the case MGM v. Grokster, *which was pending at the time it was written, Armey argues that it is important to protect the rights of intellectual property owners. Downloading music, movies, and software without paying for their use is stealing, he contends, and the peer-to-peer (P2P) network Grokster not only turns a blind eye to illegal downloading, but also actively encourages it in order to make money on advertising revenues. In Armey's opinion, if this is not stopped, creators of music, art, literature, and software will not be able to earn a living even if their works are popular and will have no incentive to take risks to create new works. Moreover, the United States cannot expect other nations to crack down on piracy of American intellectual property unless it does so at home, he maintains.*

The imperative to protect the rights of property owners is something the founding generation of Americans understood. They understood it as a moral value and as an economic necessity for any nation that sought to be strong, free and prosperous.

The founders also understood that the definition of property, and the attendant rights, could not be limited to those tangible things such as currency, livestock, homes, manufactured goods or any other things that individuals might own. Creations of the mind and imagination—music, art, literature, scientific discovery and inventions—were the hallmarks of a free and growing society, were property and had to be protected.

Article I, Section 8 of the Constitution reads: [Congress shall have the power] "To promote the Progress of Science and useful Arts, by securing for limited Times to Authors and Inventors the exclusive Right to their respective Writings and Discoveries."

They rightly understood that the real engine of economic growth for America would be the creative brilliance of the American people. And they knew that those products of the intellect and imagination were more vulnerable to theft and exploitation than a tangible piece of property that one could see being stolen. To put it more simply: It would be harder to miss someone walking off with your horse than to see someone walking off with your song. As someone raised on country and western music, I am particular to protecting both quarter horses and music.

And as an economist, former congressman, co-founder of Freedom Works and champion of the rights of property owners, I am watching with keen interest the actions of the Supreme Court in the case of *MGM [Metro-Goldwyn-Mayer-Studios] v. Grokster.*

Grokster is a peer to peer (P2P) network that allows members to "share" songs, movies, software and other creative works without paying for them.

Downloading Is Stealing

Taking something for free that you would otherwise have to pay for is called stealing. You can't walk into a store and take a music CD, a DVD movie or software for a computer game without paying for it. Yet every day, tens of millions of copyright-protected songs, movies, computer games and other pieces of intellectual property are downloaded for free—stolen over Grokster and other similar P2P networks.

Grokster doesn't just turn a blind eye to the theft—what I'd call willful ignorance—but encourages it in order to make millions of dollars in advertising revenues each year based on the number of people who steal copyright-protected property. There is little dispute that more than 90 percent of the activity that Grokster profits from is illegal. And their profits rise in direct proportion to the amount of theft. That's a racket worthy of [fictional TV crime boss] Tony Soprano.

Grokster could employ technology to stop the theft of copyrighted material, but it refuses to do so because that would force it to compete in the free market with legitimate networks like Napster, Movielink and Cinema Now that offer music, movies and games at a fair market price. But illegitimate networks such as Grokster make it almost impossible for those legitimate businesses to compete.

While millions of songwriters, screenwriters, artists, technicians, recording engineers, movie technicians and others are the individual victims of this massive, ongoing theft, the damage to our culture and to the free market economy that has made America the beacon of freedom and opportunity is immeasurable.

If the Supreme Court does not stop Grokster from engaging in and promoting these activities, the message to our children is that—should they strive to turn their dreams into music, art, literature or software—they may not be able to earn a living, even if their creations are wildly popular. The message to the rest of the world: The United States will not protect intellectual property from techno-thieves.

A Crackdown on Piracy

Intellectual property is one of America's leading exports. In times when the United States already has an enormous trade deficit, we can hardly stand by and let our innovation be stolen in broad daylight over the Internet. For example, how can we ask other nations to crack down on software piracy if we don't try to stop intellectual property theft here at home? We can't unless we want to be laughed at by the Asian, Eastern European and Middle Eastern nations where piracy of American intellectual property is rampant.

Throughout our nation's history, it has been the dreamers, the risk takers, the most creative individuals who fueled the engine of our prosperity. American ingenuity made the American economy the envy of the world. If Grokster is permitted to continue its activities, it will kill the incentive for many of those risk takers to invest in their dreams.

Our marketplace in creative property will no longer be a place where competition spurs ingenuity and benefits the consumer. And America will no longer be the land of unlimited opportunity unless you happen to run a racket like Grokster.

"File sharing gives accomplished artists
. . . a chance to control distribution of
their work that might no longer be
deemed worthy of commercial promotion and sales."

Some Artists Believe File-Sharing Networks Help Them

Jonathan Krim

Jonathan Krim is a staff writer for The Washington Post. *In the following article about the case* MGM v. Grokster, *which was pending when it was written, Krim reports that some musicians and artists do not agree with the entertainment industry's opposition to file-sharing networks. These artists do not want such networks to be shut down because these networks give their work exposure and bring them fans who might otherwise never hear of them, many of whom pay to see them in concert. Before file-sharing existed, distribution of music was controlled by large record companies, and young artists had a small chance of being signed by a record label, but file sharing gives them a worldwide audience, Krim relates. Also, it makes it possible for established artists to distribute work that is no longer being sold commercially. Advocates of file sharing claim that in opposing it, the entertainment industry simply wants to protect its monopoly, which is threatened by the existence of a nearly free distribution system.*

A prominent group of musicians and artists, breaking with colleagues and the major entertainment studios, is urging the Supreme Court not to hold online file-sharing services responsible for the acts of users who illegally trade songs, movies and software.

The group, which includes representatives of Steve Winwood, rapper Chuck D and the band Heart, said in court papers to be filed today that it condemns the stealing of copyrighted works. But it argues that popular services such as Grokster, Kazaa and others also provide a legal and critical alternative for artists to distribute their material.

"Musicians are not universally united in opposition to peer-to-peer file sharing" as the major records companies claim, according to a draft of the group's court filing. "To the contrary, many musicians find peer-to-peer technology . . . allows them easily to reach a worldwide online audience. And to many musicians, the benefits of this . . . strongly outweigh the risks of copyright infringement."

The arguments are a stark counterweight to an aggressive push by the major recording and movie studios, and hundreds of musicians, actors and composers, to persuade the Supreme Court that file sharing damages the livelihoods of artists by robbing them of proper compensation for their work.

Specifically, the studios want the court to rule that Grokster is liable for the file sharing by many of its users because it is primarily used for piracy and because it does not take steps to prevent it. . . .

Robbing Artists of Exposure

But the artists opposing the industry's position said shutting down the major file-sharing services, which are used by tens of millions of people worldwide, would instead rob them of a chance to gain exposure and income.

Before online file sharing, "distribution of recordings to retailers was controlled largely by a few large national record companies and by several 'independent' labels," they argue. "Young people aspiring to be musicians faced daunting odds of ever being signed by a record label."

One musician, Jason Mraz, said half of the fans who pay to see him in concert heard about him through illegal downloading, according to the court filing.

Meanwhile, file sharing gives accomplished artists, such as Janis Ian, a chance to control distribution of their work that might no longer be deemed worthy of commercial promotion and sales, the group said.

Attorneys for Grokster argued in its court filing that file-sharing services are used extensively for distributing works legally, either by permission of the artist or because copyrights have expired or were never sought.

As a result, the company argues, it meets the legal standard set by the Supreme Court in 1984, when it ruled that Sony Corp.'s Betamax television recorder was not liable for copyright infringement because it had substantial legal uses.

The entertainment industry's position also was opposed today by other file-sharing firms, major telecommunications companies, electronics makers, and coalitions of computer scientists, inventors, consumer and digital-rights advocacy groups.

They argue that holding technology creators, or the companies that handle Internet traffic, liable for the acts of their users would make it too risky for innovators to develop products that have legal uses and which enhance the enjoyment of digital entertainment.

New Restrictions on Innovation

"This case is simply the latest in a long string of instances in which copyright owners, frightened by a new technological development" seek to place restrictions on electronic devices, Internet access services, and even on personal computers to try to prevent piracy, said a filing by the major telephone, wireless and Internet service providers.

Instead, said companies including SBC Communications Inc. and Verizon Communications Inc., the entertainment industry can properly continue to sue individual file-swappers who break the law.

The Recording Industry Association of America has sued more than 6,500 people, and announced another 753 suits [February 28, 2005], including against some Grokster users.

The telecommunications companies also said Congress should decide how to punish services that exist solely to encourage and enable piracy.

The Distributed Computing Industry Association, which represents file-sharing and other technology firms, said the entertainment industry's real agenda is to protect its monopoly.

Grokster "threatens that monopoly by providing a near cost-free distribution mechanism, which supports far more content than even Web-based distribution systems," the group said.

Other groups filing briefs in support of Grokster's position include the Consumer Electronics Association, the Computer & Communications Industry Association, Consumers Union, the Consumer Federation of America, and Public Knowledge, a digital-rights advocacy group.

"Legal liability will interfere with the legitimate use of P2P file-sharing software and have the ultimate effect of stymieing technology."

Holding Companies Liable for Users' Copyright Violations Discourages Internet Technology

Heather S. Hall

At the time the following article was written, Heather S. Hall was a student at the Brandeis University School of Law. In the article, she explains the criteria under which the producer of software can be found liable for copyright infringement by the users of that software. In the case of MGM v. Grokster, *the circuit court applied the precedent set by* Sony v. Universal Studios *and held that Grokster was not liable because its software was capable of noninfringing uses and it had no control over what the users did. The Supreme Court reversed this decision and held that Grokster was liable because it deliberately encouraged infringement. In Hall's opinion, this ruling was a mistake. If the developers of Internet technology had been aware of the possibility of being held liable for the actions of users, the Internet might not be what it is today, she argues, and the creation of that possibility will change the way people use the Internet by ending the distribution of peer-to-peer software.*

Heather S. Hall, "Chalk Talk—The Day the Music Died," *Journal of Law and Education*, July 1, 2006. Copyright © Jefferson Law Book Company July 2006. Reproduced by permission.

Beginning with Napster, computer file-sharing software has created a unique obstacle for the recording industry in preventing copyright infringement. The [2005] *Metro-Goldwyn-Mayer Studios, Inc. v. Grokster Ltd.* Supreme Court decision (hereinafter *Grokster III*) makes it clear that distributors of computer file-sharing software can be held liable for copyright infringement committed with their software, even when they have no control over the infringement. The software distributed by the defendants in *Grokster* allowed users to exchange files via a peer-to-peer network (P2P), a decentralized system where users download from other users without using a central indexing system controlled by the software distributors. The Ninth Circuit's *MGM, Inc. v. Grokster, Ltd.* decision (hereinafter *Grokster II*) had found that the P2P software distributors were not secondarily liable for copyright infringement. Previously, courts had held P2P software distributors secondarily liable for the copyright infringement committed by software users. Although the Ninth Circuit in *Grokster II* reached a different result, it applied existing doctrine to do so. The Ninth Circuit arrived at the correct result and should not have been overturned by the Supreme Court. To understand the full significance of the decision, a basic understanding of computer file-sharing is necessary. This article will discuss the history of P2P file-sharing litigation, why the Ninth Circuit's decision was correct, and what the Supreme Court's reversal of *Grokster II* means for the future of P2P file-sharing litigation.

Computer File-Sharing and Secondary Liability

In computer file-sharing, there are three methods of indexing available files: (1) a centralized indexing system maintaining available files on one or more centralized servers; (2) a completely decentralized indexing system in which each computer maintains a list of files available on that computer only; or (3) a "supernode" system, in which a select number of computers act as indexing servers. The distributors in Grokster use a completely decentralized indexing system. When users search for a file, they are searching individual computers, not a database controlled by the distributor of the software. This is known as peer-to-peer file-sharing.

Copyright infringement occurs whenever any of the exclusive rights granted to copyright owners through the federal Copyright Act are violated. It allows for two separate theories of secondary liability, contributory infringement and vicarious infringement. To find a defendant liable for contributory infringement, a plaintiff must prove: (a) there was direct infringement by a primary party; (b) the defendant had knowledge of the infringement; and (c) the defendant materially contributed to the infringement. To analyze whether a defendant had knowledge of the infringement, courts look at whether the product is capable of substantial non-infringing use. If the product is not capable of substantial non-infringing use, courts impose a standard of constructive knowledge. If the product is capable of substantial non-infringing use, the courts employ a stricter standard of reasonable knowledge of specific infringement.

To find a defendant liable for vicarious infringement, a plaintiff must show: (a) there was direct infringement by a primary infringer; (b) there was a direct financial benefit to the defendant derived from the infringement; and (c) the defendant had the right and ability to supervise the infringers. The Ninth Circuit found that the distributors of the software in Grokster were not liable under either theory. Because the software was capable of substantial, non-infringing use, the court applied the standard of reasonable knowledge of specific infringement when determining liability for contributory infringement. According to the Ninth Circuit, the software distributors did not have reasonable knowledge of specific infringement. Therefore, they were not liable under a theory of contributory infringement. The Ninth Circuit also held that the Grokster defendants were not liable under vicarious liability because they did not have the right and ability to supervise the infringers.

Applying Existing Doctrine

The Ninth Circuit's decision in *Grokster* did not create a new standard for analyzing secondary liability for distributors of software. The court applied the doctrine created in *Sony Corp. of America v. Universal Studios, Inc.* In *Sony*, the court was faced with the question of whether the sale of Video Tape Recorders to consumers made Sony secondarily liable for the consumers' subsequent infringement. The court found there was no on-going relationship between Sony and the infringer at the time of the infringement, and therefore, there was no secondary liability. What *Sony* did was to modify liability to include a tool of infringement and apply the "staple article of commerce" rule to copyright infringement. The "staple article of commerce" doctrine says that "a product need only be capable of substantial non-infringing uses" in order for a distributor to avoid secondary liability. In other words, if the software can potentially be used in a way that does not infringe a copyright, the distributors of the software are not liable for any infringement that takes place with the software.

In *A & M Records, Inc. v. Napster, Inc.*, the court applied the doctrine created in *Sony* to peer-to-peer computer file-sharing software. Napster allowed users to access music and media files online by a centralized form of indexing, with several indexing servers. The distinction between *Sony* and *Napster* is that Napster's relationship with a consumer did not end at the point of sale, as it does when the distributor is selling a Video Tape Recorder (VTR). While Sony did not have control over the use of their VTRs, Napster maintained the right to bar a user from continued use of their software for any reason. Because the centralized indexing system allowed Napster to have actual knowledge of specific infringement and control over the infringement, the court found that the "staple article of commerce" defense did not apply, and Napster was liable for contributory and vicarious infringement.

Ninth Circuit's Decision Correct

Unlike *Napster*, the software in *Grokster* used a decentralized form of indexing that allowed users to connect with other users and search for specific digital files. Napster's software and centralized indexing allowed the distributor to control and filter user's files, but the defendants in Grokster did not maintain such control.

Applying the "staple article of commerce" defense used in *Sony*, the Ninth Circuit decided that the Grokster distributors should be held to a standard of reasonable knowledge of specific infringement. The distributors were not held liable because their knowledge fell short of this standard. If Grokster shut down all databases they controlled, their users would be able to continue sharing files with each other because indexing was not controlled by the defendant. Although the distributors conceded that the majority of the files exchanged through their software were in violation of copyrights, the court said this was not sufficient knowledge. Because the distributors lacked knowledge, the court was correct in finding no liability for contributory infringement.

In determining vicarious infringement, the decentralized indexing employed by the defendants means that the control was vested in the users of the software, not the software distributors. Because the Grokster distributors lacked the right and ability to supervise the infringers, the court was correct in finding no liability for vicarious infringement. The end result of *Grokster II* was that if a defendant's actions involved only distribution of software capable of substantial, non-infringing uses, then they were not liable for contributory or vicarious infringement.

The Ninth Circuit's decision led many scholars to call for a stricter analysis for determining secondary liability in P2P software cases. However, there are many policy reasons why the Ninth Circuit was correct in its analysis of peer-to-peer file-sharing and the secondary liability of software distributors. P2P software shaped the Internet as we know it today. If Internet service providers were initially aware of the possibility of being held liable for online copyright infringement, the Internet might not be the wealth of ideas it is today. P2P software also enables free speech and, as such, should be afforded a certain level of protection.

Supreme Court's Reversal

The Supreme Court held that a distributor of a device, who has the object of promoting its use to infringe copyright, as shown by clear expression or other affirmative steps taken to encourage infringement, is liable for the resulting acts of infringement by third parties. In reversing the Ninth Circuit's holding, the Supreme Court's decision created a new theory for finding secondary liability, which it labeled the inducement rule. The inducement rule requires courts to inquire into a software distributor's intent when determining whether the distributor should be secondarily liable for copyright infringement.

By applying a new theory to the determination of secondary liability for software distributors, the Supreme Court attempted to create clarity in a confusing area of the law. However, the Court was unsuccessful in its efforts. The Supreme Court has only added more fuel to the fire by applying the inducement rule and allowing the existing *Sony* test to apply where a product is used to infringe but there is no evidence of intentionally inducing the infringement.

The Supreme Court's decision attempted to balance artistic protection and advances in technology, but incorrectly decided that artistic protection takes priority. The Ninth Circuit correctly balanced these interests and determined that allowing distributors of P2P software to be held secondarily liable for users' copyright infringement was inconsistent with existing doctrine. The Ninth Circuit attempted to clarify an area of law that is murky at best. The Supreme Court's reversal only adds more confusion and fails to create a clear standard for finding distributors of P2P software secondarily liable for copyright infringement.

The software in Grokster was capable of substantial, non-infringing use. The Ninth Circuit acknowledged that the illegal use of the software was not sufficiently more harmful than the legal use was beneficial. Copyright law is important, but in *Grokster II* the Ninth Court correctly recognized that it is not always paramount to other societal interests. If software distributors are held secondarily liable, society would likely miss out on the benefits of P2P file-sharing software. Essentially, distributors are only indirectly responsible for any copyright infringement. Copyright holders can pursue other methods of enforcement, such as law suits against individual users and encryption programs for computer files.

The *Grokster III* decision essentially makes it easier to hold software distributors legally liable for users' copyright infringement. Legal liability will interfere with the legitimate use of P2P file-sharing software and have the ultimate effect of stymieing technology. Grokster makes it clear that P2P file-sharing software is a permanent fixture, not a temporary one, in Internet use. Creating liability for the software distributors will effectively end the distribution of a lot of P2P software, and ultimately, change the way people use the Internet. The Supreme Court's reversal of the Ninth Circuit has opened the door to possible litigation for use of P2P software and the future does not look promising for continued use of the technology.

"The copyright industry's legal toolkit to challenge developers of p2p file-sharing technologies is only marginally greater now than before the Supreme Court decided [MGM v. Grokster]."

The *Grokster* Decision Will Not Prevent the Development of File-Sharing Technology

Pamela Samuelson

Pamela Samuelson is a professor at the University of California–Berkeley with a joint appointment in the School of Information and the School of Law. She is also codirector of the Berkeley Center for Law and Technology. In the following viewpoint, she explains that the outcome of MGM v. Grokster *was not what MGM really wanted, even though it won the case. The entertainment industry had hoped that the Supreme Court would overturn the decision it made in* Sony v. Universal Studios, *which provided a "safe harbor" for technology developers whose products were used for copyright infringement if the product was capable of substantial noninfringing uses. Instead, it ruled merely that developers could be held liable for copyright infringement if they had actively induced illegal copying—which Grokster had done. Therefore, software developers can go on producing file-sharing software as long as they are careful not to promote it in such a way as to imply that it is intended for illegal use. In Samuelson's opinion this is good news for technology innovators in general, as they will not have to worry about being sued if their products are used illegally by people whom the creators have not encouraged to do so.*

MGM's [Metro-Goldwyn-Mayer Studios'] media blitz has given the impression that the entertainment industry won an overwhelming and broad victory against peer to peer (p2p) file sharing and file sharing technologies when the Supreme Court announced its decision in the *MGM v. Grokster* case on June 27, 2005. MGM can, of course, point to the 9-0 vote that vacated the Ninth Circuit Court of Appeals' decision that Grokster could not be charged with contributory infringement because it qualified for a safe harbor established by the Supreme Court in 1984 in its *Sony v. Universal* decision. The safe harbor protects technology developers who know, or have reason to know, that their products [videocassette recorders in the case of *Sony*] are being widely used for infringing purposes, as long as the technologies have, or are capable of, substantial noninfringing uses (SNIUs). The Court in *Grokster* saw no need to revisit the *Sony* safe harbor. However, it directed the lower courts to consider whether Grokster actively induced users to infringe copyrights, a different legal theory.

MGM didn't really want to win *Grokster* on an active inducement theory. It has been so wary of this theory that it didn't actively pursue the theory in the lower courts. What MGM really wanted in *Grokster* was for the Supreme Court to overturn or radically reinterpret the *Sony* decision and eliminate the safe harbor for technologies capable of SNIUs. MGM thought that the Supreme Court would be so shocked by the exceptionally large volume of unauthorized up- and downloading of copyrighted sound recordings and movies with the aid of p2p technologies, and so outraged by Grokster's advertising revenues—which rise as the volume of infringing uses goes up—that it would abandon the *Sony* safe harbor in favor of one of the much stricter rules MGM proposed to the Court.

These stricter rules would have given MGM and other copyright industry groups much greater leverage in challenging disruptive technologies, such as p2p software. Viewed in this light, MGM actually lost the case for which it was fighting. The copyright industry's legal toolkit to challenge developers of p2p file-sharing technologies is only marginally greater now than before the Supreme Court decided the case. . . .

Had Grokster won before the Supreme Court, MGM and copyright industry groups would have gone immediately to Congress to insist on technology-hostile legislation akin to [the 2004] INDUCE [Inducing Infringement of Copyrights] Act. There would have been a big fight between the technology industry and the entertainment industry over what the legislation should look like, but legislation would almost certainly have ensued. Frankly, any law that would have come out of that sausage factory would have been a lot less technology-friendly than the *Grokster* decision the Supreme Court issued. Thus, the narrow victory MGM won before the Supreme Court has deprived it—for now—of its strongest argument for legislation to put p2p and other disruptive technology developers out of business. Insofar as MGM's goal in the *Grokster* case was to persuade the courts or the Congress to give it much stronger legal protection, it has not succeeded.

Justice Souter for the Court

All nine Justices joined the *Grokster* opinion written by Justice [David] Souter. The opinion begins with the Court's statement of the question presented by the case: "under what circumstances [is] the distributor of a product capable of both lawful and unlawful use liable for acts of copyright infringement by third parties using the product." (Compare this to the question that MGM had asked the Court to address: "Whether the Ninth Circuit erred in concluding . . . that the Internet-based 'file sharing' services Grokster and Streamcast should be immunized from copyright liability for the millions of daily acts of copyright infringement that occur on their services and that constitute at least 90% of the total use of the services." MGM had been hoping that the Court would say that the *Sony* defense didn't apply to "services" such as Grokster's and that the estimated 90% of infringing uses on Grokster's p2p system attested to by MGM's expert was intolerable.)

Souter succinctly stated the Court's conclusion: "one who distributes a device with the object of promoting its use to infringe copyright, as shown by clear expression or other affirmative steps taken to foster infringement, is liable for the resulting acts of infringement by third parties." The Court accepted that the *Sony* decision had limited technology developer liability insofar as it was predicated on the design of an infringement-enabling technology, its distribution, and uses made of it, but "where evidence goes beyond a product's characteristics and uses, and shows statements or actions directed to promoting infringement, *Sony*'s staple-article rule will not preclude liability."

The Court drew upon patent law for this principle. Active inducers of patent infringement cannot escape liability by showing that they are selling a technology suitable for non-infringing uses. However, merely selling a technology suitable for non-infringing uses does not establish active inducement of patent infringement. The Court, thus, borrowed patent law's staple article of commerce rule in *Sony*, and its active inducement rule in *Grokster*.

Concerning evidence of inducement, the Court said that "the record was replete with evidence that from the moment Grokster and Streamcast began to distribute their free software, each one clearly voiced the objective that recipients use it to download copyrighted works, and each took active steps to encourage infringement." Streamcast, for example, "monitored both the number of users downloading its program and the number of music files they downloaded" and promoted Streamcast's software "'as the #1 alternative to Napster.'"

Streamcast's executives "aimed to have a larger number of copyrighted songs available on their networks than other file-sharing networks" and provided users with the ability to search for "Top 40" songs. Grokster "sent users a newsletter promoting its ability to provide particular copyrighted materials."

Problems with Inducement Claims

Grokster and Streamcast sought to avoid liability for "bad" facts such as these by, in effect, bifurcating the lawsuit into "then" and "now" time periods. Grokster and Streamcast asked the lower court to rule that they qualified for the *Sony* safe harbor as to *current* versions of their software. Grokster and Streamcast were hoping that evidence of earlier misconduct wouldn't spill over to the more recent period during which they had arguably cleaned up their acts. A successful *Sony* safe harbor defense as to current technologies would mean that these defendants could continue to operate while the legal proceedings dragged on as to earlier versions of the software and other conduct. Money damage awards subsequently imposed as to earlier versions of the software might eventually force them to shut down, but a successful *Sony* defense would give them an opportunity to sell ads to feed to their users in the meantime. . . .

Insofar as the Ninth Circuit's ruling in favor of Grokster could be construed as precluding liability for current versions of the defendants' software on any secondary liability theory because Grokster's software was capable of SNIUs, the Court decided that the Ninth Circuit had interpreted *Sony* too broadly.

MGM is not all that keen to pursue inducement claims against developers of p2p and other infringement-enabling technologies. Although copyright law does not have a secondary liability provision, it was foreseeable that when presented with an appropriate copyright inducement case, courts would borrow an inducement liability standard from patent law, just as the Supreme Court had borrowed the safe harbor for SNIU technologies from patent law in *Sony*. The burden of proof that standard requires will often be difficult for the entertainment industry to meet. Patent law requires proof of overt acts of inducement, such as advertising that actively promotes infringing uses or instruction manuals that show users how to infringe, as well as proof of a specific intent to induce infringement. Plus, there must be underlying infringing acts that were induced by this defendant. Merely making or selling an infringement-enabling technology will not suffice, even if the technology is widely used for infringing purposes. The public interest in access to its non-infringing uses is protected by the SNIU safe harbor. Moreover, some caselaw and commentary support the proposition that active inducers can continue to sell technology with SNIUs after they stop overt acts of inducement.

MGM is concerned that developers of p2p software will articulate a plausible substantial non-infringing use, such as downloading open source software, for their technologies and will be careful not to say anything that directly encourages infringing uses. MGM believes that they will nonetheless secretly intend to benefit from infringing uses that ensue. If there are no overt acts of inducement and no proof of specific intent to induce infringement, and if the *Sony* safe harbor continues to shield technology developers from contributory liability, MGM will find itself on the losing side of challenges to technology developers for infringing acts of their users. That is why MGM didn't really want to win the *Grokster* case on this theory.

The Future of Safe Harbor

Although the Court was unanimous about remanding the case to consider active inducement, the Justices appear to be in three camps about the *Sony* safe harbor for technologies with SNIUs. Justice [Ruth Bader] Ginsburg, writing a concurring opinion for herself and Justices [Anthony] Kennedy and [William H.] Rehnquist, questioned whether there was sufficient evidence in the record to conclude that Grokster's software had or was capable of SNIUs. Her opinion suggests that she construes the *Sony* safe harbor more narrowly than other Justices. Justice [Stephen] Breyer, writing for himself and Justices [John Paul] Stevens and [Sandra Day] O'Connor, used his concurrence to explain why he supports preserving the *Sony* safe harbor. . . .

Justice Ginsburg agreed with MGM that *Sony* was a very different case than *Grokster* and that the *Sony* decision did not unequivocally establish blanket immunity for technologies capable of SNIUs. . . . Justice Ginsburg questioned whether the evidence really established, as the lower courts had opined, that Grokster had and was capable of non-infringing uses. While she did not endorse the "primary use" standard of contributory liability for which MGM argued, Justice Ginsburg seems willing to leave less breathing room for developers of infringement-enabling technologies than other members of the Court.

Justice Breyer accepted that Grokster had qualified for a *Sony* safe harbor defense to charges of contributory infringement because of the SNIUs the technology had and was capable of. His concurrence mainly considered whether "MGM has shown that *Sony* incorrectly balanced copyright and new-technology interests." He posed three further questions to inform his answer to the larger question: "(1) Has *Sony* (as I interpret it) worked to protect new technology? (2) If so, would modification or a strict interpretation significantly weaken that protection? (3) If so, would new or necessary copyright-related benefits outweigh such weakening?"

Justice Breyer concluded that *Sony* did indeed protect new technologies "unless the technology in question will be used *almost exclusively* to infringe copyrights." The *Sony* safe harbor "shelters VCRs, typewriters, tape recorders, photocopiers, computers, cassette players, compact disc burners, digital video recorders, MP3 players, Internet search engines, and peer-to-peer software," although not cable descramblers. The latter may be theoretically capable of non-infringing uses, but they do not have and are not capable of plausible SNIUs. The *Sony* safe harbor is good in part because it is clear and in part because it is forward-looking. "It does not confine its scope to a static snapshot of a product's current uses (thereby threatening technologies that have undeveloped future markets)," citing VCRs as an example of a technology whose uses evolved considerably over time. Moreover, the *Sony* safe harbor avoids ill-informed judicial second-guessing of technology design decisions.

Justice Breyer concluded that modifications of the *Sony* safe harbor "would significantly weaken the law's ability to protect new technology." Requiring technology developers to produce "business plans, profitability estimates, projected technological modifications, and so forth" would increase "the legal uncertainty that surrounds the creation or development of a new technology capable of being put to infringing uses." Innovators "would have no way to predict how courts would weigh the respective values of infringing and non-infringing uses; determine the efficiency and advisability of technological changes; or assess a product's future market." Because copyright law requires imposition of statutory damages [payment per work instead of actual losses], even in the absence of actual damages—which range from $750 to $30,000 per infringed work—"the price of a wrong guess" could be so costly that technological innovation would be chilled by the prospect of immense damage awards.

Justice Breyer found most difficult his third question about whether benefits to copyright owners from a modification of *Sony* outweighed the new technology interests that the *Sony* safe harbor had thus far protected. While "a more intrusive *Sony* test would generally provide greater revenue security for copyright holders," it was less clear that "the gains on the copyright swings would exceed the losses on the technology roundabouts." . . . Although unauthorized p2p copying probably had diminished copyright industry revenue, Breyer noted that studies of the effects of p2p file sharing were unclear on the extent of harm and on whether creative output had diminished. Moreover, lawsuits against individual file-sharers appear to be having some deterrent effects, and there is evidence of a steady migration of users to licensed services such as iTunes. In view of these factors, Breyer concluded that MGM had not made a persuasive case for modifying the *Sony* safe harbor.

Good News for Developers

The Court's decision not to revisit the *Sony* safe harbor for technologies having or capable of SNIUs is very good news for the technology community. This aspect of the Court's decision is, in itself, a considerable defeat for MGM and the entertainment industry which believed the "bad" facts of the *Grokster* case would be compelling enough to induce the Court to reinterpret *Sony*. . . .

As long as the courts apply high standards for inducement liability—requiring proof of overt acts of inducement, underlying acts of infringement, and a specific intent to induce infringements—there should be ample room for innovative technologies to continue to thrive. Engineers will need to watch what they say during the development process, and firms will need to think carefully about how they should go about building markets for their products and services. But shouldn't they be exercising such care even without the Court's guidance about inducement liability?

Of course, the entertainment industry will try to make as much out of some loose language in the Court's opinion as it can; for example, as to inferring intent to induce infringement from technology design choices and from revenue sources that can in some way be linked to infringement. I submit that these efforts will fail in the absence of strong evidence of intent from other sources. Judges are not well-suited to second-guess technology design decisions, nor are they well-suited to decide what business models firms should have adopted. It would be inconsistent with patent caselaw and *Grokster*'s reaffirmation of *Sony* for courts or juries to infer intent to induce from the provision of technologies or services that have or are capable of SNIUs, even those widely used for infringement. Justice Souter's opinion has many positive things to say about the advantages of p2p technologies and about the *Sony* safe harbor, even if not about Grokster and Streamcast.

In view of these considerations, I question how much of a "win" *Grokster* really was for MGM. It certainly did not win the case in the way and to the extent it hoped. The *Sony* safe harbor survived a tough challenge before the Supreme Court, and this is good news for the technology community and for the public.

Organizations to Contact

The editors have compiled the following list of organizations concerned with the issues debated in this book. The descriptions are derived from materials provided by the organizations. All have publications or information available for interested readers. The list was compiled on the date of publication of the present volume; the information provided here may change. Be aware that many organizations take several weeks or longer to respond to inquiries, so allow as much time as possible.

Center for the Study of the Public Domain (CSPD)
Duke University Law School, Durham, NC   27708-0360
(919) 613-7270 • fax: (919) 668-0995
e-mail: jenkins@law.duke.edu
Web site: www.law.duke.edu/cspd

The center is devoted to promoting research and scholarship on the contributions of the public domain to speech, culture, science, and innovation, as well as debate about the balance needed in the U.S. intellectual property system. Its site contains information on its projects and articles by professors and law students.

Chilling Effects Clearinghouse
e-mail: questions@chillingeffects.org
Web site: www.chillingeffects.org

A joint project of the Electronic Frontier Foundation and Harvard, Stanford, University of California–Berkeley, University of San Francisco, University of Maine, George Washington School of Law, and Santa Clara University School of Law clinics, the clearinghouse aims to help citizens understand the protections that the First Amendment and intellectual property laws give to online activities. Its site offers background material and explanations of the law for people whose Web sites deal with topics such as fan fiction, copyright, domain names and trademarks, anonymous speech, and defamation. Its focus is a database of "cease and desist" notices (C&Ds) sent by copyright holders to Internet users, with legal interpretation of those notices.

Copyright Society of the U.S.A. (CSUSA)

352 Seventh Ave., Ste. 739, New York, NY 10001
Web site: www.csusa.org

A not-for-profit corporation, the society serves as a center of the U.S. copyright community for business people, lawyers in private practice and in-house, law professors, and law students who share a common interest in copyright and related intellectual property rights. It works to advance the study and understanding of copyright law and related rights. It offers answers to questions about copyright, an archive of past newsletters, and a Copyright Kids site for younger readers.

Creative Commons

171 Second St., Ste. 300, San Francisco, CA 94105
(415) 369-8480 • fax: (415) 278-9419
Web site: http://creativecommons.org

A nonprofit corporation, Creative Commons is dedicated to making it easier for people to share and build upon the work of others, consistent with the rules of copyright. It provides free licenses and other legal tools to mark creative work with the freedom the creator wants it to carry, so others can share, remix, or use it commercially. Its site has extensive information about the concept, including many videos.

Digital Future Coalition (DFC)

1341 G St. NW, Ste. 200, Washington, DC 20005
(202) 628-9210
e-mail: dfc@dfc.org
Web site: www.dfc.org

The Digital Future Coalition is committed to striking an appropriate balance in law and public policy between protecting intellectual property and affording public access to it. The organization is the result of a unique collaboration of many of the nation's leading nonprofit educational, scholarly, library, and consumer groups, together with major commercial trade associations representing leaders in the consumer electronics, telecommunications, computer, and network access industries. Its online archives include congressional bills related to the issues with which it deals.

Electronic Frontier Foundation (EFF)
454 Shotwell St., San Francisco, CA   94110-1914
(415) 436-9333 • fax: (415) 436-9993
Web site: www.eff.org

The leading civil liberties group defending the rights of the public in the digital world, the Electronic Frontier Foundation, in the area of intellectual property, fights to preserve balance and to ensure that the Internet and digital technologies continue to empower citizens as consumers, creators, innovators, and scholars. Its site contains detailed discussion of court cases involving copyright, such as *Sony v. Universal Studios* and *MGM v. Grokster*, including complete archives of legal documents.

Home Recording Rights Coalition (HRRC)
e-mail: info@hrrc.org
Web site: www.hrrc.org

The Home Recording Rights Coalition is an organization originally formed at the time of the *Sony v. Universal Studios* case to work toward reversal of the decision disallowing home recording on VCRs, which was overturned by the Supreme Court. Its site contains legal documents and background information on that case and several others, including the Digital Millennium Copyright Act.

Library Copyright Alliance (LCA)
Web site: www.librarycopyrightalliance.org

A coalition of five major library associations representing more than eighty thousand information professionals and thousands of libraries of all kinds throughout the United

States, the members of the Library Copyright Alliance cooperate to address copyright issues that affect libraries and their patrons. Its site contains news, policy statements, and contact information for each of the five associations.

Motion Picture Association of America (MPAA)

1600 Eye St. NW, Washington, DC   20006

(202) 293-1966 • fax: (202) 296-7410

Web site: www.mpaa.org

The Motion Picture Association of America is the voice and advocate of the American motion picture, home video, and television industries. Its Web site contains an antipiracy section including information about who piracy hurts and how to fight it.

Public Knowledge

1875 Connecticut Ave. NW, Ste. 650, Washington, DC   20009

(202) 518-0020 • fax: (202) 986-2539

e-mail: pk@publicknowledge.org

Web site: www.publicknowledge.org

A Washington, D.C.–based public interest group working to defend citizens' rights in the emerging digital culture, Public Knowledge's Web site contains explanations of current copyright issues, among others; a copyright tutorial for musicians; and a blog.

QuestionCopyright.org

544 Guerrero St. #2, San Francisco, CA   94110

e-mail: editors@questioncopyright.org

Web site: http://questioncopyright.org/

A nonprofit organization devoted to questioning the idea that copyright is necessary for the promotion of creative expression. Its site contains many articles and links plus several videos.

Recording Industry Association of America (RIAA)

1025 F St. NW, 10th Fl., Washington, DC 20004
(202) 775-0101
Web site: www.riaa.org

The trade group that represents the U.S. recording industry, the Recording Industry Association of America's mission is to foster a business and legal climate that supports and promotes its members' creative and financial vitality. Its Web site contains a downloadable guide titled "Young People, Music and the Internet," as well as news about its efforts to combat piracy, information for parents, and a list of legal music sites. There is also a FAQ for students doing reports.

United States Copyright Office

101 Independence Ave. SE, Washington, DC 20559-6000
(202) 707-3000
Web site: www.copyright.gov

The federal government's office handling copyright applications, the copyright office offers basic information about copyright law plus a FAQ list, a video, historical information, congressional testimony, and a section for students and teachers titled "Taking the Mystery Out of Copyright."

World Intellectual Property Organization (WIPO)

34, chemin des Colombettes, Geneva 20 1211
  Switzerland
+41 22 338-9111 • fax: +41 22 338-9070
e-mail: mail@wipo.int
Web site: www.wipo.int

A specialized agency of the United Nations, World Intellectual Property Organization is dedicated to developing a balanced and accessible international intellectual property (IP) system, which rewards creativity, stimulates innovation, and contributes to economic development while safeguarding the public interest. Its site offers the comprehensive downloadable booklet *Understanding Copyright and Related Rights*, as well as extensive resources for all aspects of intellectual property and a special section for students featuring comic books that explain copyrights, trademarks, and patents.

For Further Research

Books

Keith Aoki et al., *Bound by Law? Tales from the Public Domain*. Durham, NC: Duke University Press, 2008.

Cheryl Bensenjak, *Copyright Plain and Simple*. Franklin Lakes, NJ: Career Press, 2001.

Michele Boldrin and David K. Levine, *Against Intellectual Monopoly*. New York: Cambridge University Press, 2008.

David Bollier, *Brand Name Bullies: The Quest to Own and Control Culture*. Hoboken, NJ: Wiley, 2005.

James Boyle, *The Public Domain: Enclosing the Commons of the Mind*. New Haven, CT: Yale University Press, 2008.

Henri J.A. Charmasson and John Buchaca, *Patents, Copyrights and Trademarks for Dummies*. Indianapolis: Wiley, 2008.

Joanna Demers, *Steal This Music: How Intellectual Property Law Affects Musical Creativity*. Athens: University of Georgia Press, 2006.

Cory Doctorow, *Content: Selected Essays on Technology, Creativity, Copyright, and the Future of the Future*. San Francisco: Tachyon Press, 2008.

Stephen Fishman, *Public Domain: How to Find and Use Copyright Free Writings, Music, Art and More*. Berkeley, CA: Nolo Press, 2008.

John Gantz and Jack B. Rochester, *Pirates of the Digital Millennium: How the Intellectual Property Wars Damage Our Personal Freedoms, Our Jobs, and the World Economy*. Upper Saddle River, NJ: Prentice Hall/ Financial Times, 2005.

Tarleton Gillespie, *Wired Shut: Copyright and the Shape of Digital Culture*. Cambridge, MA: MIT Press, 2007.

Paul Goldstein, *Copyright's Highway: From Gutenberg to the Celestial Jukebox*. Stanford, CA: Stanford University Press, 2003.

Michael H. Jester, *Patents and Trademarks Plain and Simple*. Franklin Lakes, NJ: Career Press, 2004.

David Kusek and Gerd Leonhard, *The Future of Music: Manifesto for the Digital Music Revolution*. Boston: Berklee Press, 2005.

David Lange and H. Jefferson Powell, *No Law: Intellectual Property in the Age of an Absolute First Amendment*. Stanford, CA: Stanford Law Books, 2008.

J.D. Lasica, *Darknet: Hollywood's War Against the Digital Generation*. Hoboken, NJ: Wiley, 2005.

Lawrence Lessig, *Free Culture: How Big Media Uses Technology and the Law to Lock Down Culture and Control Creativity*. New York: Penguin, 2004.

———, *Remix: Making Art and Commerce Thrive in the Hybrid Economy*. New York: Penguin, 2008.

Jessica Litman, *Digital Copyright*. Amherst, NY: Prometheus Books, 2006.

John Logie, *Peers, Pirates, and Persuasion: Rhetoric in the Peer-to-Peer Debates*. West Lafayette, IN: Parlor Press, 2006.

Matt Mason, *The Pirate's Dilemma: How Youth Culture Is Reinventing Capitalism*. New York: Free Press, 2008.

Kembrew McLeod, *Freedom of Expression: Resistance and Repression in the Age of Intellectual Property*. Minneapolis: University of Minnesota Press, 2007.

Arthur R. Miller and Michael H. Davis, *Intellectual Property: Patents, Trademarks and Copyright in a Nutshell*. St. Paul, MN: Thomson West. 2007.

Neil Weinstock Netanel, *Copyright's Paradox*. New York: Oxford University Press, 2008.

Adam Thierer and Clyde Wayne Crews Jr., eds., *Copy Fights: The Future of Intellectual Property in the Information Age*. Washington, DC: Cato Institute, 2002.

Siva Vaidhyanathan, *Copyrights and Copywrongs: The Rise of Intellectual Property and How It Threatens Creativity*. New York: New York University Press, 2003.

Periodicals

Michael Abrams, "Einstein Inc.," *Discover*, March 2008.

American Libraries, "J.K. Rowling Wins Copyright Fight," October 2008.

Brooks Boliek, "Grokster Case Fit to Be Tried," *Hollywood Reporter*, June 28, 2005.

Susan Butler, "Sony Betamax Precedent Will Be Put to Test," *Billboard*, April 2, 2005.

Susan Butler et al., "Grokster Bad, Music Industry Good," *Billboard*, July 9, 2005.

Tamara Conniff, "Lawyers Swap Arguments to Decide Fate of Napster," *Hollywood Reporter*, October 3, 2000.

K. Matthew Dames, "Why Copyright Isn't Property," *Information Today*, February 2009.

Robert Darnton, "Google and the Future of Books," *New York Review of Books*, February 12, 2009.

Economist, "A Bad Week for Pirates," July 2, 2005.

———, "Face the Music," April 2, 2005.

Andrea L. Foster, "Professors Join the Fray as Supreme Court Hears Arguments in File-Sharing Case," *Chronicle of Higher Education*, April 8, 2005.

Ben Fritz and William Triplett, "High Noon for Digital Players," *Daily Variety*, March 28, 2005.

Michael Goldfarb and Theresa H. Segall, "Personalities," *Washington Post*, January 27, 1982.

Scott E. Graves, "The Supreme Court at the Technology Frontier: Brand X and Grokster," *Justice System Journal*, September 1, 2006.

Heather Green and Susann Rutledge, "Does She Look Like a Music Pirate?" *BusinessWeek*, May 5, 2008.

Linda Greenhouse, "High Court Sustains Ford Memoir Copyright; High Court Holds Magazine Violated Copyright," *New York Times*, May 21, 1985.

———, "Justices Get Case on Ford Memoirs; Unauthorized Publication of Excerpts Pits Press Rights Against Copyright Law," *New York Times*, November 7, 1984.

———, "The Supreme Court: Protected Works; 20-Year Extension of Existing Copyrights Is Upheld," *New York Times*, January 16, 2003.

Wendy M. Grossman, "Flagging Copy Rights," *Scientific American*, September 2005.

Al Kamen, "Court Rules Magazine Violated Copyright," *Washington Post*, May 21, 1985.

Steven Levy, "The Supremes Hit the Pirate Ships," *Newsweek*, July 11, 2005.

———, "A Very Dangerous Supremes Rerun," *Newsweek*, April 4, 2005.

Arnold H. Lubasch, "Trial over Article on Ford Memoirs Nears a Close," *New York Times*, January 28, 1982.

David Margolick, "Trial over Article on Ford Memoirs Begins Today," *New York Times*, January 25, 1982.

Paul Marks, "Copyright Crimes and Misdemeanours," *New Scientist*, July 5, 2008.

Sarah McBride, "For Grokster, It's the Day the Music Died," *Wall Street Journal*, November 8, 2005.

Sarah McBride et al., "Music Industry to Abandon Mass Suits," *Wall Street Journal*, December 19, 2008.

George H. Pike, "The Future of P2P," *Information Today*, September 2005.

————, "Google, YouTube, Copyright, and Privacy," *Information Today*, April 2007.

Catherine Rampell, "Antipiracy Campaign Exasperates Colleges," *Chronicle of Higher Education*, August 15, 2008.

Amy Schatz et al., "Grokster, Streamcast Can Be Sued over Piracy," *Wall Street Journal*, June 28, 2005.

Andrew L. Shapiro, "Copyright Monopolies," *Nation*, February 17, 2003.

Seth Shulman, "Freeing Mickey Mouse," *Technology Review*, November 2002.

Time, "Crackdown in the Living Room," November 2, 1981.

————, "Decision: Tape It to the Max," January 30, 1984.

William Triplet, "Grokster Ruling Stirs Dissent," *Daily Variety*, July 14, 2005.

————, "Senators Are Perplexed by P2P Decision," *Daily Variety*, July 29, 2005.

William Triplet and Ben Fritz, "Grokster Logs Off," *Daily Variety*, November 8, 2005.

Tom Zeller, "As Piracy Battle Nears Supreme Court, the Messages Grow Manic," *New York Times*, February 7, 2005.

Index

A

Ambrister, Trevor, 95
A & M Records v. Napster (2001),
152, 176–177
Anderson, Sherwood, 137–138
Armey, Richard K., 165–168
Artists
    benefits of file-sharing net-
      works for, 169–172
    harm to, from piracy, 16
    incentives for, 146–148
    selling of rights by, 14–15
Ashcroft, Eldred v. (2003). See El-
    dred v. Ashcroft (2003)
Associated Press, International
    News Service v. (1918), 84
Authors
    economic effect on, of home
      taping, 48–49
    heirs of deceased, 17
    home taping violates rights of,
      46–48
    incentives for, 146–148
    limit on control of, 84
    selling of rights by, 14–15
Authors League of America, 46

B

Band, Jonathan, 52–63
Berkman Center for Internet and
    Society, 135–136, 139
Betamax, 20, 23–24
    See also Videocassette record-
      ers (VCRs)

Blackmun, Harry
    dissenting opinion by, in Sony
      v. Universal Studios, 33–44,
      62
    draft opinion by, in Sony v.
      Universal Studios, 54–60
    support for Sony's petition by,
      53
Bollier, David, 144–150
Bono, Mary, 147
Bono, Sonny, 113, 131, 138
Book distribution, 15
Book excerpts
    fair use and, 70–71, 74, 79–93
    from A Time to Heal, 70–71,
      79–93, 97–98, 102, 107
Book publicity, 110–111
Bradbury, Ray, 141
Brennan, William J.
    dissenting opinion by, in
      Harper & Row v. Nation,
      82–93, 97, 103, 108, 111
    on Sony v. Universal Studios,
      56–57, 62
Breyer, Stephen
    dissenting opinion by, in El-
      dred v. Ashcroft, 124–133,
      149
    on MGM v. Grokster, 186–188
Burger, Warren, 53

C

Campbell, Donna M., 137
Classic works
    distribution of, 126–127
    Eldred's Web site on, 136–138,
      145

Clinton, Bill, 138

Clinton, Hillary Rodham, 105–106, 109–110

Commercial interests, protection of, 94–100

Community Television of Southern California v. Gottfried (1983), 31

Companies, as rights holders, 14–15

Congress
   authority of, to extend copyright, 116–117, 122–123, 149
   role of, in responding to new technologies, 26–28, 56

Conrad, Joseph, 140–141

Contributory infringement
   finding of, 29, 40
   guerrilla video sites and, 66, 67–68
   liability for, 41–42, 55, 175, 177
   standard for, 62

Copyright
   debate over, 15–17
   duration of, 116–120, 139–140, 147
   as incentive to create, 146–148
   information dissemination and, 103–104
   limitations on, 83–84
   literary, 17, 141
   new technologies and, 26
   news value and, 75
   purpose of, 30, 35, 73, 76, 83

Copyright Act (1976)
   fair use and, 97–98
   intention of, 34–35, 56, 63
   originality requirement in, 83
   rights conferred by, 37, 46–47, 74
   time-shifting and, 59–61

Copyright clause, 14, 116–119, 121–123, 125–126

Copyright infringement
   companies' liability for users', 173–179
   contributory, 29, 40–42, 55, 62, 66–68, 175, 177
   file-sharing services are liable for, 154–164, 182–184
   home taping as, 33–44
   secondary, 158, 174–179, 184–185
   unlawful objective and, 162–163
   vicarious, 175–176, 177

Copyright Term Extension Act (CTEA)
   constitutionality of, 115–123
   does not serve purpose of copyright, 144–150
   First Amendment and, 121–122
   intention of, 17
   lack of public benefits from, 130–131
   opposition to, 113–114, 134–143
   passage of, 17, 113
   purpose of, 113
   supporters of, 142
   as unconstitutional, 124–133, 147, 148–149
   See also Eldred v. Ashcroft (2003)

Copyrighted works
   illegal downloads of, 64–68
   market value of, 37–39, 43
   noncommercial use of, 29–30

D

Daily News (newspaper), 106, 109–110
Digital Millennium Copyright Act, 138
Distributed Computing Industry Association, 172
Dornin, Chris, 135
Dover Publications Inc., 139

E

E-book publishing, rights protection and, 17
Eldred, Eric, 114, 135–143, 145
Eldred v. Ashcroft (2003)
    case overview, 113–114
    dissenting opinion in, 124–133
    majority opinion in, 115–123
    negative reaction to decision in, 149–150
    See also Copyright Term Extension Act (CTEA)

F

Fahrenheit 451 (Bradbury), 141
Fair use
    affirmation of, 149
    book excerpts and, 70–71, 74, 79–93
    Copyright Act and, 97–98
    determination of, 35–37, 77–81, 105–111
    home television taping as, 19–20, 23, 31–32
    home television taping is not, 45–51
    market effects and, 80–81, 92–93
    news value and, 75–77, 87–90
    scholarship and, 35–36
    time-shifting as, 31–32, 40–42, 57, 158–159
    time-shifting violates, 42–44, 61
    unpublished works and, 79, 90
Fairness in Music Licensing Act, 121
FCC, Turner Broadcasting System, Inc. v., 121
Feist Publications Inc. v. Rural Telephone Service Co. (1991), 118
File-sharing services
    application of *Sony v. Universal Studios* to, 158–161
    are liable for copyright infringement, 154–164, 182–184
    benefits of, 169–172
    legal debate over, 152–153
    negative impact of, 165–168
    should not be liable for users' violations, 173–179
    See also Illegal downloads; *Metro-Goldwyn-Mayer Studios, Inc. v. Grokster, Ltd.* (2005)
File-sharing technology
    impact of *Grokster* decision on, 180–189
    types of, 174–175
First Amendment
    copyright limitations and, 84
    CTEA and, 120–122, 125, 140
    news value and, 75–77
    purpose of, 103
First publication right, 73–74, 79, 106–107, 110–111

Ford, Gerald
  distinctive expression by, 80
  memoirs of, 70–93, 95, 102,
    107
  newsworthiness of, 75, 87
  privacy interests of, 90
  See also A Time to Heal (Ford)
Foster, Andrea L., 134–143
Free speech, 120–122
Frost, Robert, 137–138
Fuld, Stanley, 76

G

Gershwin, George, 113, 127
Ginsburg, Ruth Bader
  majority opinion by, in *Eldred
    v. Ashcroft*, 115–123, 149
  on *MGM v. Grokster*, 185–186
*Gottfried, Community Television of
  Southern California v.* (1983), 31
Green, June L., 140
Grokster
  encouragement of theft by,
    167–168
  file-sharing system used by,
    175, 177
  liability of, for copyright in-
    fringement, 152–164, 177–
    179, 183–184
  support for, 171–172
*Grokster, Ltd., Metro-Goldwyn-
  Mayer Studios, Inc. v.* (2005). *See
  Metro-Goldwyn-Mayer Studios,
  Inc. v. Grokster, Ltd.* (2005)
Guerrilla video sites, 65–68

H

Haig, Alexander, 87
Hall, Heather S., 173–179
Hamilton, Marci, 64–68

*Harper & Row, Publishers v. Na-
  tion Enterprises* (1985)
  analysis of decision in, 101–
    104
  case overview, 70–71
  dissenting opinion in, 82–93
  economic interests as primary
    consideration in, 94–100
  impact on journalism of, 99–
    100
  implications of, 106–109
  majority opinion in, 72–81
  reasons for decision in, 108–
    109
*Harry Potter and the Order of the
  Phoenix* (Rowling), 106, 109–
    110
Hawthorne, Nathaniel, 136–137,
    145
Home television taping
  authors' rights and, 46–48
  as copyright infringement,
    40–42
  debate over, 52–63
  economic effect of, 48–49
  as fair use, 19–20, 23, 31–32
  impact on market value of,
    37–39, 43
  program production impact
    of, 50
  Supreme Court decision on,
    19–21
  as violation of copyright law,
    33–44
  as violation of fair use, 45–51
  *See also Sony Corporation of
    America v. Universal City
    Studios* (1984)
Howells, William Dean, 137

I

Ideas
  vs. form, 86–87
  lack of copyright on, 84–86
Illegal downloads
  impact of *Sony v. Universal Studios* on, 64–68
  liability for, 154–164
  of music, 16–17
  negative impact of, 165–168
  problem of, 152
  as theft, 167–168
  See also File-sharing services
Inducement rule, 159–161, 178, 181, 184–185
Inducing Infringement of Copyrights (INDUCE) Act, 182
Information
  free dissemination of, 94–100, 103–104
  lack of copyright on, 84–86
  See also Newsworthy information
Innovation, restrictions on, 171–172
Intellectual property (IP)
  definition of, 14
  laws, 14, 26
  protection of, 168
  See also Copyright
International News Service v. Associated Press (1918), 84
Inventors, selling of rights by, 14–15

J

Jaszi, Peter, 147

K

Kaczynski, Theodore J., 140
Karp, Irwin, 45–51
Kirkpatrick, David D., 110
Krim, Jonathan, 169–172

L

Laws
  copyright, 103–104
  intellectual property, 14, 26
Lawsuits, against file-swappers, 172
Lessig, Lawrence, 136, 142, 147, 148
Libraried copies, 67
Literary copyrights, 17, 141
Literary form
  copyright protection on, 83, 84
  vs. ideas, 86–87
Living History (Clinton), 106, 109
Luck's Music Library Inc., 139

M

Market impact
  fair use and, 80–81, 92–93
  of time shifting, 60–61
Marshall, Thurgood, 53, 60–61, 103
McLaughlin, Andrew J., 52–63
Melville, Herman, 137
Metcalf, Slade, 94–100
Metro-Goldwyn-Mayer Studios, Inc. v. Grokster, Ltd. (2005)
  application of *Sony v. Universal Studios* to, 158–161, 176, 186–187
  case overview, 152–153

development of file-sharing technology and, 180–189
dissenting opinions on, 171–172
implications of, 174, 177–179
as narrow victory for entertainment industry, 181–182, 188–189
unanimous decision in, 154–164, 182–184
Mickey Mouse, 113, 145
Morpheus, 156, 162
Motion pictures
  copyright protection on, 34
  illegal copies of, 65
  libraried copies of, 67
  preservation of old, 129
  production of, 50
Mraz, Jason, 171
Music distribution, 15, 170–171
Music downloads. *See* Illegal downloads
Musicians, benefits of file-sharing networks for, 169–172

N

Napster, 65–66, 156, 161–162
Napster, A & M Records v. (2001), 152, 176–177
Nation Enterprises, Harper & Row v. (1985). *See Harper & Row, Publishers v. Nation Enterprises* (1985)
The Nation (magazine)
  article published by, 70–81, 96–98, 102, 107
  did not violate fair use, 82–93
  lawsuit against, 96–97
  news reporting by, 87–90
  profit motive of, 102

  violated copyright, 72–81
  See also Harper & Row, Publishers v. Nation Enterprises (1985)
Navasky, Victor, 79, 80, 96, 97
Nesson, Charles R., 136
New York Times Co. v. Sullivan (1964), 84
Newsworthy information
  copyright on, 72–81
  dissemination of, 71, 98–100
  fair use and, 75–77, 87–90
  scooping of, 96–97
Nixon, Richard M., 83

O

O'Connor, Sandra Day
  on Copyright Term Extension Act, 148
  on First Amendment, 103
  majority opinion by, in *Harper & Row v. Nation,* 72–81, 96, 108
  on *Sony v. Universal Studios,* 53, 58–59, 60, 62
OpenNap, 156, 161–162
Orbison, Roy, 121

P

Paraphrase, 85
Parody, 121
Patents, 14, 183
Peer-to-peer (P2P) networks, 152–153, 174
  See also File-sharing services
Permissions, difficulty in obtaining, 17, 127–130
Person, Leland S., 137

Piracy
  crackdown on, 168
  harm from, 16
  impact of *Sony v. Universal Studios* on, 64–68
  software, 168
  See also Illegal downloads
Powell, Lewis, 53
Private property rights, 102, 104, 141, 166
Public domain, 15, 138, 141, 146
Publicity campaigns, 110–111
Publishers, 14, 15

R

Reader's Digest (magazine), 95–96
Record labels, 14
Recording industry, 16–17, 172
Rehnquist, William, 53, 58, 60, 186
Reno, Janet, 139
Right of first publication, 73–74, 79, 106–107, 110–111
Rowling, J.K., 106, 109–110
Royalties, 14, 126–127
Rural Telephone Service Co., Feist Publications Inc. v. (1991), 118

S

Safe harbor protection, 181, 184–188
Samuelson, Pamela, 180–189
Scientific progress, 119–120, 126, 166
Secondary liability, 158, 174–179, 184–185
The Secret Agent (Conrad), 140–141
Self-publishing, 15

Shafer, Jack, 105–111
Software piracy, 168
Sondheim, Stephen, 47
Sonny Bono Copyright Term Extension Act. *See* Copyright Term Extension Act
Sony Corporation
  liability of, for copyright infringement, 39–40
  VCRs produced by, 19–20, 23–24
Sony Corporation of America v. Universal City Studios (1984)
  amicus curiae brief in, 45–51
  application of, to file-sharing services, 153, 158–161, 176, 186–187
  case overview, 19–21
  Court of Appeals' decision in, 24–25, 46
  debate over, 52–63
  dissenting opinion in, 33–44
  impact of, on illegal downloading, 64–68
  majority opinion in, 22–32, 89
  See also Home television taping
Souter, David, 154–164, 182–184
Staple article of commerce rule, 176, 177
Stevens, John Paul
  draft opinion by, in *Sony v. Universal Studios*, 53–59
  majority opinion by, in *Sony v. Universal Studios*, 22–32, 62–63
StreamCast
  liability of, for copyright infringement, 152–164, 183–184

OpenNap program of, 156, 161–162
Sullivan, New York Times Co. v. (1964), 84

T

Technologies
    legislative response to new, 26–28
    restrictions on, 171–172
    safe harbor protection and, 181, 185–188
Television programs
    illegal copies of, 65
    libraried copies of, 67
    production of, 50
    time-shifting of, 28–32
Television taping. *See* Home television taping
Time (magazine)
    cancellation of contract by, 92, 96, 102, 107
    contract between Harper & Row and, 70, 79–81, 95–96
A Time to Heal (Ford)
    book excerpts from, 70–71, 79–93, 97–98, 102, 107
    copyright on, 70, 72–81
    nature of, 78–79
    rights to, 95
    similarities between *Nation* article and, 85–86
    See also Harper & Row, Publishers v. Nation Enterprises (1985)
Time-shifting
    adverse effect of, 37–39
    authorized, 28–29
    Copyright Act and, 59–61
    as copyright infringement, 40–42

economic impact of, 60–61
    as fair use, 31–32, 40–42, 57, 158–159
    unauthorized, 29–31
    value of, 56
    as violation of fair use, 42–44, 61
Trademarks, 14
Turner Broadcasting System, Inc. v. FCC, 122

U

Universal City Studios, Sony Corporation of America v. (1984). *See Sony Corporation of America v. Universal City Studios* (1984)
Unpublished works, 79, 90
U.S. Constitution, copyright clause of, 14, 116–119, 121–123, 125–126

V

Valenti, Jack, 147–148
Vicarious infringement, 158, 175–177
Video rental business, 20, 62–63
Videocassette recorders (VCRs)
    introduction of, 19, 34
    liability of manufacturers of, 39–40
Videotape recorders (VTRs). *See* Videocassette recorders (VCRs)

W

Walt Disney Company, 113, 145–146
Webster, Noah, 130

White, Byron, 57–58, 60, 103
Will, George F., 101–104
Work for hire, 14

Z

Zittrain, Jonathan L., 135, 136